Gerald Be

religious philosophy. After teaching religious studies and philosophy in colleges and universities in Britain, he moved to France. He is the author of several other books for Watkins and he has won awards for a novel, several short stories, and radio drama for the BBC World Service.

By the Same Author

Watkins Dictionary of Religions and Secular Faiths

The Mayan Prophecies for 2012

Sacred Texts: Celtic Wisdom

Sacred Texts: The Song of Songs and the Psalms

Sacred Texts: Buddhism

Sacred Texts: Chinese Wisdom

THE MAYA

2012:

THE END OF THE WORLD OR THE DAWN OF ENLIGHTENMENT?

GERALD BENEDICT

WATKINS PUBLISHING
LONDON

This edition first published in the UK and USA 2010 by
Watkins Publishing, Sixth Floor, Castle House,
75–76 Wells Street, London W1T 3QH

1 3 5 7 9 10 8 6 4 2

Designed and typeset by Jerry Goldie

Printed and bound in China

Library of Congress Cataloging-in-Publication Data Available

ISBN: 978-1-907486-59-3

www.watkinspublishing.co.uk

For
Noémie and Amélie,

Fame is rot; daughters are the thing.

J M Barrie

CONTENTS

Acknowledgements ix
Introduction xi

Part I: Remembering the Future

1 Time, Prophecy, and the Mayan Prophecies 3
2 The Chilam Prophets 9
3 The Prophecies 13

Part II: Time – and Time Again

4 The Lines and Circles of Time 45
5 'The Great Influence of Time' 50
6 Understanding the Times 72

Part III Getting it Together

7 'A Most Unique Conjuction' 80
8 Playing the Cosmic Game 87
9 Conjunctions and Correlations 98
10 The Menaces from Space 109

Part IV: Who On Earth Are We?

11 Creation and Its Myths 121
12 We only Know in Part 147

Part V: What Will the Future Bring?

13 'This is the Way the World Ends' 161
14 Redeeming the Time 178
15 Prophecy and Evolution 186

Part VI: 2012 and Beyond

16 The Enduring Message 200

References and Further Reading 215

ACKNOWLEDGEMENTS

During the writing of this book, I have been fortunate to have had the help and guidance of several people. Something of a 'day-keeper' himself, huge thanks are due to my editor, Michael Mann, for his astute advice and encouragement, and to his team of editors, copy-editors and designers.

I am very grateful for the contribution my daughters have made; Amélie, for table talk about finite element analysis, thus ensuring that I properly understood the relationship between linear and circular time, and Noémie, for her line-drawing of the ball court, carefully extrapolated from various sources. My wife, Nadège, has been endlessly encouraging and indispensably supportive, holding us together by her patience and humour.

For advice, information, and permission to use their work, I'm indebted to Jacob Rhythmic Dragon, Director of Communications at the Foundation for the Law of Time (www.lawoftime.org and www.13moon.com), to Valum Votan (Dr José Argüelles), to David A Dundee, Director and Chairman of the Fernbank Science Centre Planetarium, to Jean Molesky-Poz and the University of Texas Press for material from her excellent and important book, *Contemporary Mayan Spirituality*, and to the journal, *Alternate*

Perceptions, for the use of Bruce Scofield's concise summary of the 'personalities' of the *katuns*. I want, especially, to thank my friends Richard and Susan Nethercott, and Peter and Julie Smith, whose conversations have helped clarify my thinking and made me aware of things I'd not seen. My friend and clarinet teacher, Remko Wellerdieck, knows as much about harmony as did the Mayan astronomers; his company and lessons, and playing jazz with him, have helped me keep the beat going during the past few months. I am particularly grateful to Michael D Jacobson, always available to read work in progress, and to guide and advise.

I have made every effort to secure permission to reproduce material protected by copyright, and will be pleased to make good any omissions brought to my attention in future printings of this book.

Gerald Benedict, Payrignac, France

INTRODUCTION

The Maya are attracting a great deal of attention. There are three principal reasons for this, the first being the approach of the end date of their Long Count calendar, 21 December 2012; the second, that at sunrise on that date, with the cycle of precession completed, there will be an alignment of the planets, the Earth, Sun and Milky Way, which only happens every 26,000 years; and thirdly, that the message of the Mayan prophecies is intended for those of us who are living during the years leading to and beyond 2012.

Mayan history is customarily divided into the Pre-Classic Period, approximately 2000 BCE–250 CE, the Classic Period, 250–900 CE, and the Post Classic Period, 900–1521 CE. What follows is the Spanish conquest and its influence on every aspect of Mayan life and culture. Earlier, towards the end of the 9th century, the Maya were said to have 'disappeared'. This was because, in central and southern Yucatán, many of the main sites were abandoned and quickly reverted to jungle. The decline was rapid, and its causes continue to be debated. The various theories suggested include some form of major catastrophe such as an earthquake or disease; more likely is the decline of agriculture, with its consequent crop failure, and the threat of imminent famine, causing the population to move elsewhere.

At its height, Mayan civilization was the most sophisticated and advanced in Mesoamerica. The Maya developed a complete hieroglyphic language, texts of which decorated the surfaces of their palaces, temples and pyramids, and were carved on to stelae. Their codices, all but a very few of which were destroyed by the Spaniards, were also written in hieroglyphics. The architecture was developed over thousands of years, the first pyramid being built at Uaxactun, in Guatemala, before the birth of Christ. The style is distinctive and spectacular, the most familiar form being the pyramid, more reminiscent of the ziggurats of Mesopotamia than the Egyptian structures. Some buildings, such as the Caracol at Chichén Itzá, were designed specifically as observatories to record the movements of a particular planet - in this case, Venus - while whole groups of buildings were arranged to align with a point on the horizon where the sun, moon, or planet would rise on a particular date. The basis of the economy was agriculture, and maize was the staple diet, the crop having considerable religious and symbolic significance. Mayan religion was a polytheistic animism, the pantheon of gods set in a hierarchy, mirroring the Maya's social structure. At the top of the pantheon was the supreme god, Kukulcan, the Mayan form of the Aztec god, Quetzalcoatl; the kings of the city states ruled over a descending order of classes and, although accorded divine rights, were held responsible for drought, crop failure and defeat in battle. The rituals and ceremonies marking the end of a significant period of time, like the 20-year *katun*, were presided over by shaman-priests who held together a holistic cosmology that believed everything to be sacred but required human sacrifice to ensure a positive relationship with the gods.

Only three codices, and fragments of a fourth, survived the Jesuit persecution. The Madrid Codex is the work of a single scribe thought to be based in the city of Tayasal, in the southern Mayan lowlands. Written after the Spanish conquest, it uses several earlier sources that have not survived. The Dresden Codex was written before the Conquest by a number of scribes, and describes rituals collated in what are known as the 'Almanacs', together with astrological tables of eclipses and the 584-day cycle of Venus. It is an important codex for Mayan astrologers. The Paris Codex records prophecies based on the *tun* and *katun* time periods, and includes a Mayan zodiac. The dates and places of origin of the Dresden and Paris codices are still debated. The 11-page fragments of the Grolier Codex came to light only in the 1970s; this offers no new material and its authenticity is in doubt. As well as the Dresden Codex, there are other sources for Mayan astrology, such the Codex Borboncius, an almanac, or *Tonalamatl*, meaning 'pages of the days'. Other than these codices, and the material gathered from the hieroglyphic texts of the archaeological sites, what we know of the Maya is dependent on the writings of Bishop Diego de Landa (1524–79) who provided a faulty but nevertheless significant contribution to the early decipherment of the Mayan writing system. His one major work, *Yucatán Before and After the Conquest*, first translated into English in 1937 by William Gates, is a detailed treatment of Mayan religion. In addition to the sources outlined above is a series of manuscripts known as the Books of Chilam Balam, or Jaguar Priests. These are scribes with special shamanic gifts and powers, who were both the receivers of the prophecies and the scribes who recorded them. The title of each book takes its name from the author and the Yucatec town where he lived. Thus we have, for example, the Book of Chilam Balam of Chumayel, others being of Mani and of Tizimin. As well as the prophecies, the shaman prophet-scribes recorded history, herbal medicine, calendrics and astrology. The Book of Chilam Balam of Chumayel includes the Book of Katun

Prophecies, i.e. prophecies associated with the recurring 20-year *katun* period. To this outline of primary sources, we need to add the *Popol Vuh*, a pre-Columbian collection of mystical histories from the Quiché region of Guatemala. The title means, 'The Book of the Community' or 'The Book of Counsel', and it was written by anonymous members of the upper classes who, as custodians of tradition, preserved the original forms of the myths. Its main theme is the creation myth, hugely important to the Maya and ever present in their consciousness.

The Maya, uniquely, held to a holistic cosmology that inextricably linked religion, astronomy, mathematics and spirituality. The prophecies perfectly express the combined force of these components and are themselves tied into the calendars and confirmed by the Mayan concept of cyclic time. The relationship between cyclic and linear concepts of time is, therefore, fully discussed. By comparing how the Egyptian, Hindu and Buddhist traditions understand time, the distinctive Mayan perception is also established. The calendars are a model of the Mayan perception of time's architecture, and each of the building-blocks used to construct the calendars is explained. The theme concludes with a discussion of the implications of applying a cyclic concept of time to our own world.

The specifics of the calendar are writ large in Mayan

astronomy, as well as the mythologies attached to it. The Maya dealt in huge periods of time – which, like the planets themselves, cycled relentlessly only to return to an original 'fixed point' every 26,000 years. The five different periods, or Suns, into which the 26,000 years was divided, all ended with some kind of catastrophe. Each separate period, whether extremely long or of just a 20-year duration, like the *katun*, has its own character, or personality, formed by the events that took place during its cycle. As the periods recur so will the events that characterize them. It therefore follows that if time cycles, so does history. The Maya applied their astronomy and concept of time to everyday life through the 'science' of astrology. While specialist shaman-priests channelled and recorded the prophecies, others practised a mundane divination, guiding and advising people in their daily lives. What kind of people they were was determined by the creation myth of the *Popul Vuh*, and something of a Mayan self-image is put together to help one understand the nature of their sense of something lacking, and their quest for wisdom. This quest, as the prophecies establish, is something shared by everyone.

What will the future bring? It will not bring the destruction of the world, but it may bring the return, in some form, of a supreme being. Certainly we will face challenging threats and great risks, some beyond our control, others within the range of our collective responsibility. Each of these is discussed in the final part of the book. The combined message of the various prophecies is positive. If we can overcome that sense of lack and recover the wisdom we have lost, we will survive by the natural process of evolution, honing those functions and faculties that will best ensure the continuation of the human race and the planet. Such survival will require the evolution of our minds, our consciousness, and our spirituality.

The themes and subjects briefly outlined above will be developed throughout the book.

Author's Note

While writing *The Mayan Prophecies for 2012*, many themes and ideas suggested themselves that were beyond the scope of that book. These have become the subjects of *The Maya, 2012: The End of the World or the Dawn of Enlightenment?* The two books stand alone, but readers of the first book will recognize 'bridge passages' taken from it, such as the summaries of the 21 prophecies in Part I, and of the basic building-blocks of the calendars in Part II. Where they have proved to be particularly apt and relevant, I have also retained some quotations and examples. I very much hope that this book will do justice to the challenging and far-reaching implications of the prophecies.

PART I

REMEMBERING THE FUTURE

Where does this difference between the past and the future come from? Why do we remember the past and not the future?

Stephen Hawking, *A Brief History of Time*

Professor Hawking's question about why we don't remember the future, that is, why we are unable to recall an event that has not yet taken place, seems paradoxical. However, it is no more so than asking the other questions he poses in his book: 'If the universe had a beginning, what happened before that?' or, 'If it has an end, what will follow it?' Many of us find ourselves pondering the size of the universe: is it actually infinite? If it is not, if the universe stops somewhere and some kind of edge limits it, what lies beyond that edge? It has been said that to speculate about such things leads to madness, driving our minds to their very real limits. Perhaps it is for this reason that Eastern meditative practices such as Zen speak of 'no mind', of transcending rational thought to the point of realizing intuitively that the answers to such questions reside in a full and true knowledge of ourselves.

— 1 —

TIME, PROPHECY, AND THE MAYAN PROPHECIES

Questions about time and the universe, and many others, become demanding the moment we try to understand the Maya's prophecies and calendars, and how these relate to their concept of time. It is the purpose of this book to explore these relationships and their implications for the winter equinox, 21 December 2012, to which the calendars point and on which the prophecies focus. Unsurprisingly, as the year approaches there is extensive interest in this subject; all eyes, as it were, are looking to 2012 as we try to fathom what is in store for us.

There is something deep within humanity's make-up that drives us to satisfy our curiosity about the future, and throughout history every culture is distinguished by its different ways of doing this. There is no limit to human ingenuity in the search for devices, rituals and systems that might provide even a glimpse of the future. In Delphi, the ancient

Greeks consulted the oracle of Apollo, a prophetess or sibyl called Pythia. Contemporary Nigerians sustain the age-old tradition of paying a Babalawo to read the Ifa oracle for them. The sages and counsellors of emperors and kings examined the entrails of animals to ascertain an auspicious time for war, trade or marriage, while millions of people today consult their daily horoscope. To know the future, people have resorted to the supernatural and paranormal: to the observation of signs and omens, to astrology and numerology, to crystal balls and palm-reading, to augury and alchemy, to rituals of divination and, with perhaps greater objectivity, to the new science of threshold and pattern dynamics.

Why then do we want to 'remember the future'? The answer is composite; part of it lies in the need for the security of that knowledge, in the hope that whatever the future will bring we will have enough control to prepare for it and avert its more negative and threatening aspects. Much of this is given over to speculation, theorizing, wish-fulfilling dreams, fantasy and a feeling of being bereft of knowledge that is part of our proper birthright. And yet a wraith of doubt haunts all such speculation. As we consider the ways in which *Homo sapiens* is different from its closest ancestors; as we give thought to the development (or, as will be explained, the evolution) of mind and consciousness; as we survey the scientific, hi-tech culture in which we have wrapped ourselves; as we consider how much of the work of our minds has been handed over to computers and machines, the haunting doubt is: are we destined or designed to know the future? Is the drive to know the future part of our karma, part of our evolving DNA – a necessary evolution if we are to survive as a species? Or is the future hidden because it is something we are not 'intended' to know, because it is 'better' for us that we don't? All these possibilities will be discussed, but in the process it is wise to heed the counsel of Marcus Aurelius: 'Never let the future disturb you. You will meet it, if you have to, with the same weapons of reason which today arm you against the present.'[1]

For the Maya, knowledge of the future was contained within their prophecies, and the form these prophecies take distinguishes them, as we shall see, from the methods and devices listed above that people have contrived in order to read what will take place in the years to come. The Mayan prophecies did not just happen, they did not suddenly appear out of the air like a new species of bird, but were an emanation of an entire culture and way of life founded on a prophetic tradition. The context for the prophecies was the Mayan understanding of time and space, something wholly abstract. The heavens were observed with the naked eye, mathematically conceived, but made visible and palpable in intricately interrelated calendars.

The idea of prophecy does not lie easily within Western, secularized culture; the prophet, an individual with a special spiritual gift, authorized to pass on the given message, is a role we ascribe to an earlier, non-scientific period when more rigid, unchallenged authorities maintained the status quo by means of fear and superstition.

There are many different kinds of prophecy and ways of prophesying. In Judeo-Christian culture the idea of prophecy has been moulded by the Old Testament tradition, in which the prophet, a person of impeccable character and religious maturity, was 'called out' by God to deliver a specific message, at a set time, to a particular people. Usually, in this tradition, the prophetic message was a warning, or admonishment, about what would happen in the future if people continued to flaunt the laws of God and refused to better their ways. The authority of the prophet lay in the means by which the message came to him as, for example, with Jeremiah who found God's words had been put into his mouth (Jeremiah 1:9) or Isaiah who volunteered, 'Here am I; send me' (Isaiah 6:8) or through an overwhelming vision such as that given to Ezekiel. This is the prophecy of consequence, of cause and effect: 'If you don't do this, then that will happen'.

More usually, prophecy is taken to indicate what will happen in the future, regardless of how we behave. It suggests a kind of predestination, or a predetermined course of events over which the way we live has no control. All we can do in response to such prophecies is make adequate preparation.

It is fair to say that the strength of a prophecy is no greater than its authority, and it is in this respect that Mayan prophecy is unique. The authority of 'true' prophecy is not founded on what inspires the prophet, or the means by which the prophecy is received and its message delivered, but in the extent to which its content adds new insight to the already received tradition. Thus, real prophecy can be thought of as a progressive evolution of an idea or perception. The meaning of the prophecy is not to be found in its most obvious character of warning, it is not a matter of cause and effect, of merely drawing attention to the consequences of present behaviour and values. The real meaning is to be found in those parts of its message that advance our spiritual maturity. This 'higher' form of prophecy will not incite fear or a knee-jerk reaction, but a response that is both eminently practical and transcendent; it will not just alert us to the urgent needs of our world and our society, but will illuminate our knowledge of ourselves; it will not only motivate us to certain courses of action, but will point us to an understanding of our place in the world and the nature of our relationship with it; it will define our shortcomings and limitations while offering a tantalizing view of our extraordinary potential, the possibilities of which we have hardly glimpsed. The Mayan prophecies are of this order. The received tradition recorded in the codices is not entirely a matter of history, it is an ongoing, vital energy to which contemporary Mayan day-keepers and elders such as Hunbatz Men, Ajq'ij Roberto Poz Perez and José Arguelles are making their own contribution.

It is important to understand that, for the Maya, their concepts of time and prophecy were the ground of their being, and the framework of their mythologies. There is no culture in the modern world that bears any resemblance to that of the Maya. A unique combination of factors gave rise to the Mayan prophetic tradition, notably an extraordinary knowledge of astronomy and mathematics; a specialized cult of priests who imparted the prophecies; and the process of receiving, transmitting and preserving these prophecies. What makes it difficult for the Western world to enter the matrix of Mayan thought is the unique relationship between religion, cosmology, astronomy, mathematics and spirituality. These combined to provide the mindset that produced the prophecies, and which is best suited for understanding and interpreting them.

— 2 —

THE CHILAM PROPHETS

The original prophets, who made up an elite priesthood, were called 'Chilam', or 'Chilan', a title to which was added the epithet 'Balam', meaning jaguar, an important figure in Mayan mythology. The jaguar, it was believed, could roam between different spiritual levels, as it does physically between day and night. Everything that lives was associated with the day; the world of the spirit and the ancestors with the night. The title or name 'Balam' was not only used by the elite priesthood but also by kings and other members of the ruling class. To 'Chilam' was added the name of the place where the priest lived, and it was by this combination that the codices are identified, for example, 'The Book of Chilam Balam of Chumayel'. The only other codices that have survived the Spanish conquest are those of Mani, Tizimin, Kaua, Ixil and Tusik. Something in the order of 13 other codices were destroyed by the Jesuits. The Maya believed the cult of Chilam priests was descended from the original order established by the god, Quetzalcoatl (*see* below, and Part V) and bestowing the title 'Chilam' indicated both their high rank and the special gifts that merited them being priests. They enjoyed a special status in Mayan society and were highly regarded and respected, being, says the Chilam Balam of Tizimin, 'the fathers of mankind'.

The priests were shamans, that is to say, they acted as mediums between the visible, tangible world, and the invisible world of the spirits, engaging in practices and rituals designed to control natural events, to heal and to prophesy. Shamanism is not a religion or cult in itself, but a spiritual tradition, not dissimilar to mysticism, a practice found within many religions. As Mircea Eliade put it, Shamanism 'is one of the archaic techniques of ecstasy – at once mysticism, magic and religion, in the broadest sense of the terms'.[2] The shaman's role is vocational and sometimes hereditary. He stands apart from the community he serves, separated by the intensity of his own spiritual experience and his unique personal communion with spirits of another world. The shaman, through dance and trance states, will descend to the underworld or rise to heaven, achieving a state of 'ecstasy', which, in this context, means the soul's release, albeit temporarily, from its physical confinement in the body.

In the Mayan tradition, the shaman Chilam delivers

'ecstatic prophecy', a transmission that virtually overcomes the prophet/god duality. What we are concerned with here is not simply a message delivered by language, but an exchange, or sharing, of a unique kind of experience. The Chilam will have had actual experience, at a refined spiritual level, of what he is given to communicate; such experiences are very persuasive. They can be thought of as the 'special branch' of a priesthood responsible for a considerable range of services which included invoking the deities; regulating the calendars; studying the night sky and interpreting the appearances, movements and relationships of the planets; reading the sacred writings and the prophetic character of the *katuns*; supervising the carving of the steles and the building of temples; and constructing tables of eclipses and the heliacal rising and setting of the planets.

The central and most important role of the Chilam was that of prophecy. One of the codices describes how the Chilam Balam of Tizimin gave his prophecy; the method is probably typical:

> He went into a room in his home and lay down, passing into a trance-like state. The communicating god or spirit, sat on the ridge of the house and spoke to the unconscious Chilam. When it was finished, other priests gathered in what may have

been the reception hall of the house, and they listened as the receiving prophet told his message. They kept their faces to the floor.[3]

— 3 —

THE PROPHECIES

In general terms the Mayan prophecies can be divided into four groups:[4] day prophecies, year prophecies, messianic prophecies and those of Pacal Votan. The day prophecies are prognostic and the concern of an *ah-kinyah*, a diviner, rather than a Chilam. Each of the 260 days of the *tzolk'in* calendar (*see* Part II) is marked by the diviner as lucky or unlucky, and he will consult the day-keeper to ascertain if the day is auspicious for agriculture, business, trade, professional occupations, etc. The year, or *katun* prophecies, are true prophecies associated with the 20-year period of a specific *katun*, thus the Katun 5 Ahau. These prophecies are like those given by the minor Hebrew prophets in that they warn of drought, famine, pestilence, war, political unrest, the destruction of towns, the captivity of people. The importance of these *katun* prophecies, which include those relating to the Maya's own history, is that they are derived from genuine and ancient sources which, in the process of translation, have not been 'interpreted' by the Spanish missionaries. The third group of prophecies speaks of the return of a supreme being, and the fourth, the prophecies of Pacal Votan, stand alone.

The following 21 prophecies fall, roughly, within these four general categories. They have been drawn from the primary sources of the Chilam Balam of Chumayel,[4] Chilam Balam of Tizimin,[5] Hunbatz Men,[6] and Pacal Votan.[7] A brief summary of each of the prophecies is given here as background to the references made to them throughout the book.

– PROPHECY 1 –

Prophecies of the Coming of Foreigners and a New Religion

The extent to which the Maya had foreknowledge of the total decline of their classical civilization towards 800 CE is uncertain, but the 16th-century destruction of their resurgent culture by the Spanish is among the clearest of their prophecies: 'Behold, within seven score years Christianity will be introduced amid the clamour of the rulers – those who violently seize the land during the katun.'[4] The general weight of the prophecy was to give early indication of sudden radical and challenging change, and a warning to prepare for it. Radical change is a theme that runs through all the prophecies that point us to December 2012. This theme, and many others, is carried by the Maya's concept of cyclic time, especially specific periods of time, such as the 20-year *katuns*. These have particular characteristics that determined the nature of the events that would recur.

– PROPHECY 2 –

The Prophecy of the Emergence of Contemporary Mayan Masters and Teachers

The core subject of the prophecy is the return of the 'initiates of the future' to the sacred land and sites of the Maya. The responsibility of this contemporary generation of masters is to enable people to have new insight and understanding, and to acquire 'cosmic wisdom'. There is, however, one crucial new element in the fulfilment of this prophecy. The teachers will not be drawn exclusively from the Maya. Initiates will be representatives of all cultures and religions, young and old, regardless of sex, race or class. 'These Masters will come from many places. They will be of many colours ... others will be aged. Some less so.'[6] Their main concerns will be the problems that have been caused by a materialistic education, the negative influences of a technocratic culture, and our almost total separation from nature. The prophecy speaks of our urgent need of these teachers who, by sharing the recovered wisdom, will lead us back to the basic but ominously neglected sources of spiritual fulfilment, and of life itself.

– PROPHECY 3 –

The Prophecy of the Return to Mayan Ceremonial Sites

Western culture's sensitivity to 'place' has been numbed by its disregard for nature and exploitation of the planet's resources. Many present-day westerners no longer sense the numinous power and holiness of the sacred sites. In this respect, India is both an exception and an example: 'India is a vast network of sacred places. The entire country is a sacred land. The sacredness of the land of India is what, still today, gives a sense of unity to this country of so many religions, cultures, races and factions.'[8] Wherever we live, and whatever path we follow, the prophecy calls us to recover our sensitivity to places charged with spiritual energy and knowledge.

— PROPHECY 4 —

The Prophecy of the Return of a Supreme Being

Contemporary Mayan elders have a somewhat different take on what the return of Quetzalcoatl - the god known to the Maya as Kukulcan, who is discussed in Part V - actually means. They confirm that a broader, rather than a literal interpretation does greater justice to the message. Rather than predicting the physical return of an ancient god, the prophecy tells us that with the

> ... initiation of cosmic wisdom people can attain the same, high spiritual state, so as to 'become' Kukulcan ... From this moment on, I would like you to realize that we are all Quetzalcoatl or Kukulcan. We need only to develop our faculties of consciousness to fully realize that status.[9]

The ideal is consistent with other religions that seek union with a divine, or ultimate being.

– PROPHECY 5 –

The Prophecies of Pacal Votan

The prophecies of the Mayan sage-king, Pacal Votan (603–683CE), stand alone, and need explanation. The prophecies were delivered post-mortem from his famous tomb in the Temple of Inscriptions at Palenque, where the king was worshipped as a god. When the tomb was discovered in 1952, the excavations uncovered a stone tube for which Dr José Argüelles coined the name 'psychoduct', or Telektonon, running from the burial chamber to the temple floor above. We are told on good authority:

> The Kings of Palenque were practical men as well as people of faith. To help their ancestors ascend to the world of humankind, they created a physical path for the Vision Serpent to follow when a dead king wished to speak to his descendants.[10]

Pacal Votan's prophecies were likely to have been transmitted in this way, mythically emanated to the priests who came to consult him and to seek his advice. The tomb and Telektonon functioned as a form of oracle, a 'talking stone of prophecies'. The Maya believe that what Pacal Votan first transmitted was the source of their knowledge of astronomy and mathematics which combined to produce the calendars that were the basis of the prophecies. Pacal Votan was also known as the 'Closer of the Cycle', thus, the prophecies point to the end of the cycle of the Long Count calendar in December 2012. These prophecies are not warnings of catastrophe, or the end of the world, but of an evolving Earth, of spiritual evolution (*see* Part V). They anticipate the extreme materialism of our age, the dangers of uncontrolled technology, and the ecological crisis. Pacal Votan's prophetic vision was, 'that humanity as a species would become disconnected from the laws of the natural world and would fall ignorant of our sacred interdependence with nature.[7]

Pacal Votan's epigram – 'All is number. God is number. God is in all' – links with the Mayan absolute, Hunab K'u, 'the Giver of Movement and Measure'. The two combine to suggest that mathematics, together with movement and measure, is the source of life. The qualities of balance, order and harmony combine to form both the spiritual life of each individual, and the physical life of the cosmos. The prophecy calls us to use personal, collective and cosmic energy to transcend the materialism and techno-dominance of our age, so as to prepare for the problematic transition into the next World Age. In this process, humanity will experience an evolutionary development of new creative and communicative faculties.

– PROPHECY 6 –

The Prophecy of Galactic Synchronization

The prophecy speaks of the energies and influences to be released as a result of a conjunction of planets that takes place, approximately, every 26,000 years. The event is called, 'galactic synchronization', which means the Earth and the solar system will be in conjunction with the rest of the universe and its plane will be in line with the plane of our galaxy, the Milky Way. The prophecy speaks of this as a sign which marks the moment of turning towards a new 'Sun' or World Age. The sign is the visible conjunction of the Sun with the Milky Way, understood by the Maya to be the Tree of Life. In more immediate terms, the most important aspect of this prophecy is that the coming galactic synchronization will produce specific 'energy' effects (*see* prophecies 16 and 17).

– PROPHECY 7 –

Prophecy Related to the Milky Way

This prophecy combines Mayan mythology and astronomy. In the mythology, the Milky Way, called the Ceiba tree, was understood as the Tree of Life. What will occur in 2012 is that the winter solstice sunrise will come into conjunction with the 'Dark Rift', the central point of the Milky Way. The prophecy of the Milky Way forming the symbolic tree-image speaks of the continued evolution of the entire planet and of everything that is dependent on it for its life, both physically and spiritually. Aware that the eventual alignment will take place at the end of the 13th *baktun* of the current cycle (*see* Part II), the prophecy anticipates a major point of transition in the history of planet Earth, the start of a new World Age, and an unprecedented creative shift in human consciousness and civilization.

– PROPHECY 8 –

Prophecy Related to the Moon

While the Maya share with many other cultures a rich and obsessive mythological attachment to the Moon, they are unique in giving the Moon its own calendar, the *Tun-Uc* (*see* Part II). The prophecy related to the cycles of the Moon's phases in the *katun* ending in 2012 carries a message that is less than positive. The Moon's character of deceitfulness, promiscuity and unpredictability suggests events that will both surprise and challenge us. The Moon's association with water implies periods of disastrously destructive flooding. The 'man in the Moon' image, so familiar to us, is seen by the Maya as 'the rabbit in the Moon' which carries the link with drunkenness, and thus of a humanity intoxicated with pleasure and materialism, but also in search of deeper satisfaction and contentment. In sharp contrast, the Moon's relationship to childbirth suggests a more positive outcome, perhaps the emergence of a new, sensitive and more cosmically conscious humanity. A practical edge is given to the prophecy through its association with weaving and agriculture. The extremes are clear; the outcome is in the balance.

– PROPHECY 9 –

The Prophecy Related to Venus

The prophecy related to Venus, specifically as it transits the Sun, speaks of a critical period of transition both for our planet and humanity. The Maya's fear of Venus is based on the planet's association with some form of major catastrophe, such as an earthquake that occurred, far back in Mayan history, at the time of Venus' rise or decline, or perhaps during its transit across the face of the Sun. Because of the concept of cyclic time and history, it was feared a similar event could recur. One of the means of averting the planet's violent and negative influences, was the practice of human sacrifice. The implication for our own, final *baktun* is that those dying in war might be thought of as having been 'offered' in sacrifice, the necessary price to be paid for the preservation of our civilization. In a broader sense, the prophecy calls for self-sacrifice, not suicide but restraint, in the face of the problems facing our society and planet. To balance this somewhat austere forecast, we can refer to that part of the build-up to galactic synchronization at the winter solstice of 2012 when, on 6 June, Venus will transit the Sun (*see* Part II). Because of the planet's association with the god Quetzalcoatl (Kukulcan) the transit is to be understood as a visible appearance of the Feathered Serpent which, for contemporary Mayan elders points to 'Cosmic Initiation' (*see* prophecy 13) and the time when the solar sunspot activity will be at its maximum, generating other forms of energy on Earth (*see* prophecy 17).

– PROPHECY 10 –

The Prophecy of Transition to a New Age

The fifth Mayan World Age is drawing to a close; the sixth will begin in 2012. This will mark the start of the new Great Cycle of time and the resetting of the clock of precession. We are, thus, between ages, periods known to the Maya as the 'Apocalypse', meaning a time of revelation or disclosure. Our transition towards a New Age offers us the chance to improve and stabilize our relationships, and to accept our responsibility for the Earth. It is only by making such positive choices that we can begin to solve the problems we face. In Mayan cosmology, the New Age signifies the creation of a new world; hopefully, this will mean regeneration for humanity and the planet's ecology.

– PROPHECY 11 –

The Prophecy of the Unity of Mankind

The message of the prophecy is stark; put simply, in the words of Benjamin Franklin, 'We must indeed all hang together, or, most assuredly, we shall hang separately.' It is prophesied that as we move towards 2012 the various races, religions and classes will be drawn closer together. The Chilam Balam of Tizimin wrote, 'I repeat my words of divine truth: I say that the divisions of the Earth shall be one!'[5] This was corroborated by a prophecy of Pacal Votan, 'I come to you as the special witness of time to remind you, especially on the day of truth, that in your origin you are one, and on the day of truth you are to make yourselves one again.'[7] Humanity is fighting its battle on two fronts, the one being to prevent the collapse of our own civilization, the other to prevent the terminal spoliation of our planet. The only possible way to resolve these problems is for a globally concerted effort to be made.

— PROPHECY 12 —

The Prophecy of a New 'Enlightenment'

This prophecy is telling us that we need to make a radical shift in our perceptions, especially with regard to our relationship with nature, and with understanding our place within the universe. The enlightenment of which the prophecy speaks includes the concept of 'awakening' to the truth, something that is also at the heart of Eastern mysticism. But the Mayan teachers do not expect this to be a matter of sudden, or immediate perception. This will certainly be the experience of some, but for most of us it will happen more gradually, through a process of teaching and reflection. It will be a gradual realization, a slow dawning that, eventually, will touch everyone. The Chilam Balam of Tizimin tells us: 'Your souls shall accept the truth and hold it in high esteem ... It will come to pass that you shall adore the divine truth ...'[5] The prospect of fulfilling such a prophecy is positive and optimistic.

— PROPHECY 13 —

The Prophecy of Cosmic Consciousness

The Maya understood that everything that exists is energy, and that consciousness is a property of matter. Thus, what appears to be a prophecy rooted in an abstract, metaphysical process is in reality, far more concrete. The Mayan elders teach that during this inter-age period, it will be the choices we make that determine how we enter the next age, and that these choices will have real and practical consequences to the point of determining not only the quality of future life, but whether there will actually be a future (*see* Part V). The prophecy speaks of the power of sharply focused collective thought which may, potentially, be the most powerful energy humankind has ever realized.

– PROPHECY 14 –

The Prophecy of Recovered Memory

The Chilam records that, 'a wave of disgust sweeps through the house of the gods because you forgot Life, you forgot your own ancient teaching'.[5] The prophecy predicts that the final *baktun* will be a period of 'great forgetting', during which our proper relationship to nature will be impaired. It also speaks of our recovery from this amnesia, as we regain the original insight and knowledge. Wisdom, or cosmic consciousness, is not the monopoly of any one culture or nation, but in history there are occasions when it is given to certain people so that they can be its custodians. When the time is auspicious, it can then be recovered. The prophecy speaks of a coming memory revolution. This recovery of knowledge 'will enable people to echo the memory of the universe. And the new humankind will possess special capabilities, rationality and emotion.'[11]

– PROPHECY 15 –

The Prophecy of the Destruction of the Earth

Among the predicted causes of an Earth-threatening catastrophe, comet impact must remain a possibility, but we have to keep in mind that while some interpretations of the prophecies point to a massive global catastrophe, comet impact is only one of several possible scenarios (*see* Part V). Other interpretations suggest more local, natural occurrences. What the prophecy speaks of clearly is that while a sudden, terminal end of the Earth is unlikely, we will have to work through the consequences of our spoliation of the planet, and of our exploitation of its natural resources. The end of each Mayan age, or Sun, is marked by extreme natural catastrophe (*see* Part III). The current age or Fifth Sun, will terminate in 2012 and it is prophesied that the Earth will experience violent earthquakes and volcanoes, huge winds and storms. The Chilam Balam of Tizimin wrote that '... in the final day of misfortune, in the final days of the tying up of the bundles of the thirteen katuns on 4 Ahau, then the end of the world shall come ...'[4] Despite this prediction, most scholars of the Mayan calendric prophecies do not support the idea that the end of world is imminent, but the consensus is that we could be in for a rough ride, and that we can expect to see 'chaos and destruction in all the kingdoms of nature'.[12]

– PROPHECY 16 –

Prophecies of Earth Changes, Ecology and Climate

The prophecy tells us that, 'the surface of the Earth will be moved ... According to the omens above the Earth and the prophecies, the disturbances of our land shall eventually turn back.'[5] The prophecy is about our pollution of the biosphere in the decades leading to 2012, which has set us in conflict rather than in harmony with nature. The crust, or shell of our planet, the air, all surface soil, sand, rock, water, in fact all those elements of the Earth that support life, are at risk. Opinion remains divided about the extent to which advances in science and technology, and the industries supported by them, have contributed to global warming and climate change. The latter, may well be part of natural cycles of change over very long periods of time. Returning this important prophecy of Earth changes back to Mayan calendric astronomy, we can say the Earth has entered the final phase, or *katun* (1992 to 2012) of the Great Cycle, a period leading to the Earth's conjunction with the Milky Way. That the 'disturbances of our land shall eventually turn back', give the prophecy an optimistic edge in that it suggests we will recover our sense of responsibility for the planet. The Maya call this the 'Earth Regeneration Period', when, as a result of the 2012 conjunction, the planet will begin to cultivate a new and complete 'purity'.

We can but hope.

– PROPHECY 17 –

The Prophecy of Changes to the Earth's Magnetic Field

The Maya prophesied a recurrence in 2012 of the conditions that may have contributed to the collapse of their civilization in the 9th century. What the prophecy speaks of is excessive sunspot activity, and changes in both the Earth's and Sun's magnetic centres. Hunbatz Men tell us that, 'thousands of years ago the sacred teachings from the cosmos were deposited in many magnetic fields throughout the world'.[6] These centres include, Chan Chan (Peru), Tulle (France), Bethlehem (Israel), Tih (Egypt), Nagasaki (Japan), and Mull (Scotland). With the NASA projections for 2012 corroborating changes in the magnetic field (*see* page 167), some form of disaster does seem likely. While the entire Earth may not be threatened we ought, perhaps, to have contingency plans in place to cope with volcanic eruptions, floods, conflagrations, earthquakes, or a combination of these. Mayan calendars were therefore pointing to 2012 as a date wrapped around by a long and gradual process of atmospheric and environmental changes, when a series of natural disasters might well cause considerable damage and suffering.

– PROPHECY 18 –

Prophecies of Evolution and Genetics

The prophecy speaks of a natural, evolutionary development of all aspects of human biological potential, from the genetic content of our DNA, to the interrelationship between human electrodynamics and the physical rhythms of the Earth. This interrelationship will, itself, be the context for the further evolution of human consciousness (*see* page 190), that is, of the brain mechanisms that sustain and operate it, and it will lead the human mind to hitherto unimagined abilities, skills and creativity. Beyond that, since consciousness is the only means we have of relating to the infinite, or absolute, its further evolution will lead us to a more mature spirituality (*see* Part V). Behind this prophecy is the Maya's insight into Hindu kundalini practice which calls up an energy that drives all human growth and development in both individual and evolutionary terms. This energy is embedded in the Mayan mythologies of Kukulcan (Quetzalcoatl) the Mayan supreme being (*see* Part V). As John Major Jenkins stated, 'the ancient Maya understood something about the nature of the cosmos and the spiritual evolution of humanity that has gone unrecognized in our own world-view'.[13] This is a wholly positive prophecy that serves us well in the face of the imminent problems we must overcome.

– PROPHECY 19 –

The Prophecy of Transcending Technology

The Chilam Balam of Chumayel points us to Katun 2 Ahau, the 12th *katun*. 'For half the katun there will be bread; for half the katun there will be water. It is the word of God. Its bread, water and temple are halved. It is the end of the word of God.'[4] Katun 2 Ahau is the first *katun* of the New Age following the winter solstice of December 2012. The key to the prophecy is the halving of the things that naturally sustained Mayan physical life, and the halving of the temple practice that sustained their spiritual life. Previous Katun 2 Ahaus have been clearly marked with physical and spiritual crises and the prophecy warns that a similar crisis is imminent. What threatens our spirituality most, and most immediately, are the consequences of a hypertechnology that is also the source of our food and medicines. We are warned that technology has exceeded the point where it serves humanity in securing a better quality of life; it has accelerated to the point where we have given ourselves over to materialistic and consumerist values; it has contributed to our severance from nature and 'natural time' (*see* prophecy 20). The scientist and ecologist Dr Charles Birch has warned that 'our technological civilization has not adapted to the needs of survival ... The sort of society we are building with the aid of science and technology has self-destructive features built into it.'[14] The prophecy calls us back to the running theme of our need to recover our natural integration with nature, and speaks of our urgent need to transcend a technology that is rapidly approaching the time when technology will transcend us (*see* Part V).

– PROPHECY 20 –

The Prophecy of Time

The Chilam Balam of Tizimin is telling us that, 'a time will come when the katun-folds will have passed away, when they will be found no longer, because the count of tuns is reunited'.[4] Time will no longer be divided, calculated or perceived in quite the same way. Thus, the prophecy speaks of our need to change the way we think about time which has been entirely conditioned by the linear forms of the Julian and Gregorian calendars. What 2012 marks is not the end of time in the sense of it being the end of the world, but the end of the conventional way we understand and experience time.

> We have thus come to comprehend that our notions of a three-dimensional Euclidean space and of linear flowing time are limited to our ordinary experience of the physical world and have to be completely abandoned when we extend this experience.[15]

By this abandonment, we shall acquire a deeper understanding and, by consequence, a deeper experience. Our awareness of these principles will gather considerable momentum towards 2012, but to change our concept of time will require a radical alteration of our perception.

– PROPHECY 21 –

The Prophecy that We Are the Prophecy

The combined weight of the prophecies points inevitably to the responsibility of those destined to live during and beyond the period of the final *katuns* of this age. The Chilam Balam of Chumayel reminds us that 'this is the record of the wisdom of the book in which is set down the course of each katun ... whether it is good or bad. These things shall be accomplished. No one shall cause them to cease.' Knowing that we are the prophecy confronts us with a question we can't avoid: what does it mean to be nearing the completion of the precession of the equinoxes, and what can we expect – personally as well as cosmically – in 2012? (*See* Part V for further discussion of this.) The truth is, we can have no expectation, we do not know what will happen, but the prophecy is positive in telling us that by the priorities we establish and the choices we make, we can determine a creative future for our civilization. Most importantly, the prophecy points to us as the agents for necessary and radical change. We cannot pass the buck.

The Maya believe the future is formed by replication and variation of what has happened in the past. Prophecy and history are thus inextricably mingled, since the record of what has happened in the past is the source for determining what will create both the present and the future. Prophecy, for the Maya, was therefore an investigation of events in future time, based on historical precedent. A dialogue between linear and cyclic time took place for the Chilam at a psychic level, the former recording the history of events, the latter carrying a recurrence of those events at some time in the future. That dialogue takes place in the present moment of the Chilam in question and, as Tedlock puts it, 'the interaction of these same two forces in present time produces a strain along the localized boundaries where one named and measured segment of time must succeed or replace another'.[24] What actually happens is that where the interaction takes place the meeting point becomes an imbrication, that is, an overlap. These overlaps occur at the end of one cycle and the beginning of another, the ending of a cycle being the most significant period. The Chilam will consider the events and energies that precede and follow the ending, since the energies of the former will spill over into the latter.

In summary, we can say that the prophecies are based on the recurrence of similar events carried by the 'character' of a recurring period of time, most importantly, the 20-year *katun* cycle. These cycles and replications are built into the calendars the Maya developed. It is thought there were at least 20 calendars, 17 of which are on record. The calendars are complex, and Part II provides a basic account of how they are constructed and linked to each other and, most importantly, why they are the carriers of the prophecies. (A detailed explanation of the calendars, and a full commentary on the prophecies can be found in my earlier book, *The Mayan Prophecies for 2012.*[23])

The Maya were not only stargazers, essentially they were a practical people, preoccupied with survival. For everyday purposes they lived, as we do, with the idea that time is linear, although mindful of mortality, they lived by the rhythms of the infinite. The past and the future were held in balance in the present by the prophecies, and since knowledge of what might happen in the future is contained in what happened in the past, they are not a form of revelation. For this reason, prophecy might well be the means by which we can remember the future.

PART II

TIME
– AND TIME AGAIN

It would be more appropriate to call the Maya world view a chronovision, … to ignore the primordial importance of time would be to ignore the soul of this culture.

Miguel Leon-Portilla

The trouble with our times is that the future is not what it used to be.

Paul Valéry

Our lives follow a cycle of events repeated in time. Even though they are less apparent in some parts of the world, the most obvious examples are the seasons marked by the equinoxes and solstices. We celebrate annual events, national holidays and festivals, many with a religious origin - such as Christmas, the Passover, Diwali and Ramadan - others secular, like the New Year and bank holidays. In a similar way we cycle through more personally significant days, the rites of passage, the anniversaries of births, deaths and weddings. These rhythms, built in by nature or custom, suggest that recurrent events are carried by a cyclic movement of time - we say, 'The holidays have *come round* again.' Despite this, we live as if time were linear, we have the sense of moving forwards from one event to the next as we thread our way from birth to death. We imagine time to be like a frequently taken train journey, the events like familiar stations, and as with the journey itself, time seems to have both a beginning and an end.

— 4 —

THE LINES AND CIRCLES OF TIME

The Maya's concept of cyclic time is graphically illustrated by their intricate and interrelated calendars and was, for them, the reality which explained the recurrence of events over both short and hugely extended periods. They knew what we sometimes concede, that history repeats itself. Our own linear perception of time is merely a device of the mind that enables us to function. It accounts for the sense we have of moving through life, we can plan our future and record our past. The clock, a means of measuring this onward progression, is a convenient aid which, for example, enables trains and aeroplanes to run systematically according to timetables, meetings to be arranged, holidays to be planned, deadlines to be met. Clocks register the passing time with relative efficiency, and the world ticks with them. It doesn't seem to matter that our time is awkwardly determined by the planet's journey round the Sun, requiring months of different lengths and the leap year to set things straight. José Argüelles[17] has suggested a far more natural calendar: the lunar year, with thirteen 28-day months amounting to a 364-day year, leaving one to be accounted for in the solar calendar system. Argüelles' solution, imaginative and creative as it is, differs radically from the traditional Mayan system, and there seems little reason for the change.

In their calendric system, the Maya established a vital relationship between cyclic and linear time. Cyclic time was, for them, the reality holding together brief periods and immense ages, the former measured by the span of human life; the latter by the massive movements of the stars and planets, which they observed with the naked eye, measuring and recording the progressive changes of the cosmos with which human life, at its best, should be synchronized. Linear time was their functional time, determined by agricultural seasons and used to measure the length of a ruler's reign, the duration of a journey or of one's own life. Despite their necessary use of linear time, the Maya knew it to be illusory and that what we register as the linear passing of time is in no way different from the incalculably long periods of cyclic time through which the universe continues to evolve. We can think of it like this: if a circle is big enough, a small section of its perimeter will be perceived as being straight. Our lives would have to last hundreds of thousands of years for us to have any sense of the greater curve of which our normal life span is an infinitesimally small part.

Stephen Hawking[18] writes of the 'arrows' of time. He suggests there are three different arrows, each representing different aspects or functions of time. The thermodynamic arrow points to the direction of time in which disorder will increase; the psychological arrow points to the direction in which we feel the passing of time, and why we can remember the past and not the future; the third, cosmological arrow, points to the expanding rather than to the contracting universe. He argues that all three arrows impinge on each other and, when they are pointing in the same direction, conditions are favourable for the development of intelligent life capable of considering these kinds of questions.

The Maya were undoubtedly conscious of the disorder inherent in the universe they observed. By this, I do not mean the physical laws which determine the birth and death of stars and which hold the whole cosmos in balanced motion. Rather, for the Maya, the disorder of the universe was mirrored in their own history: there is continuing debate among scholars about the reasons why the Maya abandoned their cities and towns in *c.*800CE; and in the 16th century came the prophesied invasion by foreigners and the Mayan conversion to an alien religion. Disorder was mirrored, too, in the prophecy which, like an arrow of time itself, pointed to a threatening culmination at the winter equinox of 2012.

The psychological arrow, pointing to the direction of time passing, is the arrow of time with which we are most familiar: we are constantly aware of time that both drags and flashes past us. The third, cosmological arrow, pointing in the direction of an expanding universe, was one the Maya could not have been aware of, as we are today. However, their extraordinary calendars and prophecies clearly indicate that they had an inkling of some form of cosmic evolution. The intricate interrelationships of these many calendars, to be considered later, demonstrates that they also understood how these various forms of time impinged on, and overlapped each other.

The Maya were obsessed with the measurement of time, especially of its very long cycles, and their ability to do this confronts us with a double mystery. Their intricate measurements were based on naked-eye astronomy; their calculations involved an extraordinary knowledge of mathematics. Clearly, astronomy and mathematics are inextricably related and neither historians nor anthropologists have discovered how the Maya acquired these skills. Even though their astronomy was based on what they observed only with their eyes, the

Maya are renowned for the precision of their calendars over very long periods during which they were able to predict the eclipses of the Sun and Moon, and the transits of Venus.

— 5 —

'THE GREAT INFLUENCE OF TIME'

There are ancient traditions, other than the Mayas', whose cultures were formed by their concept of time and whose understanding of life and the universe was based on their measurement of huge, seemingly endless periods. We need to put the Maya into the broader context of what Swami Sri Yukteswar called 'the great influence of Time'.[19] This chapter will discuss the concept of time in ancient Egyptian, Vedic and Buddhist traditions, before giving a detailed account of the Mayan calendric system. As with the Maya, these systems are complicated, and what is now described are the essential elements.

Ancient Egypt

The Egyptians were able to conceptualize linear and circular time together. An inscription says, 'Everything that exists is eternal stability and eternal recurrence.'[20] Eternal stability is represented by linear time, eternal recurrence by circular time. Both concepts are illustrated, for example, by the Sun's rising and setting, the time between which spans the length of a day, and which also symbolizes the kingship-cycle through the reincarnation of dying kings. The Egyptians had two words to describe these aspects of time: *neheh* and *djet*,[20] neither of which translates easily into English. *Neheh* comes close to a cyclical concept of time suggested, for example, by the seasons, and includes the sense of wholeness and completion. Its hieroglyph is the image of a lit oil lamp, that is, a point of light in a circle, which Assmann[21] tells us is a universal symbol of Ra, the Sun god, and thus of the Sun itself. *Djet* indicates the linear notion of time, a time that can't be repeated, like the water of a river that flows past the point where we observe it. Its hieroglyph is made up of the image of a long snake, a loaf of bread, and an island as the symbol of land. *Djet* is earthly time, the time of here and now where we live our daily lives. Used together, the two hieroglyphs and their mythology show how the Egyptians were able to hold in balance the two concepts or functions of time, endless repetition and eternal stability. Perhaps the closest English translations for the concepts of *neheh* and *djet* are 'being' and 'becoming'. Things first have to 'be', and this coming into being is fixed in a moment of time, while their 'becoming' is a process. The act of being is endlessly repeated, the act of becoming is enduringly sustained; thus, time and eternity are held in balance.

The Egyptians had both a solar and a lunar calendar. The latter mapped 360 days over three seasons of four months each. Unsurprisingly, these three seasons were determined by the cycles of the Nile known as inundation, emergence (growth) and summer (harvest). The civil calendar of the solar year marked 365 days of twelve 30-day months with 5 additional days tagged on. In contrast to the Mayan *wayeb* (*see* below), a period when the gods withdrew their support, the five additional days marked, for the Egyptians, the period when the gods were born, when the people were supposed to remain calm, showing neither joy nor sorrow. The months of the solar calendar were of three weeks, each of ten days. The heliacal rising of the star Sirius (Sothis), around 21 June, coincided with the rise of the water level of the Nile on which Egyptian agriculture and quality of life depended. It was inevitable that they chose the rising of Sirius as the first day of the year; Egyptian astronomers recorded that a full cycle of seasons would pass before the star rose again. However, the calendar took no account of the fact that every four years Sirius rose a day later, since the star's year is the same as the solar year, that is 365 days long. Their calendar, therefore, got out of sequence with both the solar year and the seasons, to the amount of one day every four years. It took 1,460 years for the rising of Sirius to cycle round to the same point on the calendar, a cycle known as the Sothic Period. Although the Egyptians were aware of this error for many years, it was only in 238 BCE that an attempt was made to avoid the 'wandering year'. Ptolemy III decreed a reformed calendar, but it was opposed by the priesthood and not adopted until 25 BCE when a reformed version of the calendar was absorbed into the Julian calendar. The ancient, original calendar has survived and, known as the Coptic calendar, is used by the Coptic Church.

Hinduism

Perhaps more than for any other tradition, the concepts of time treated by Vedic Hinduism deal in massive periods which, as with the Maya, were a part of its cosmology and creation myths. The dominant concept is, again, of time as cyclical, and time is also a manifestation of Brahma (God in his aspect as creator of the universe). The fourth of the Vedas, the Atharvaveda, tells of time being the ruler of all things: 'It is he who caused the worlds to come into being and holds them. He is the father of all things. There is no power greater than he.'[59] In the Bhagavad-Gita, Krishna, the best known of all Hindu deities, says, 'I am Time'.

The act of creation recurs along with everything else, and each newly created cycle is made up of four huge aeons: Krita (or Satya) Yuga, Treta Yuga, Dwapar Yuga and Kali Yuga. Each has a character of its own that dominates the age bearing its name. The Krita Yuga was the ideal age. There was no strife, no enmity, no hate or envy, no fear or anxiety. It is the Yuga to which the others aspire, to which they will return. The Treta Yuga was a Yuga of sacrifice and righteousness, during which the positive aspects of the preceding Yuga declined by a quarter. The people of this age hoped to be rewarded, and could gain merit by observing ceremonies and rituals, but their sense of duty and commitment declined. Righteousness was reduced by half in the Dwapar Yuga. The observance of ritual was the best means of accruing merit, but fewer people than before were interested in the truth, or sought it. As a result, desire and disease became apparent, as did injustice in all its forms.

Only one-quarter of the original, pristine righteousness survives in the present age, the Kali Yuga, which began in 3102 BCE: little interest is shown in spirituality, and what was known of it is neglected and forgotten. The age is dominated by evil tendencies, anger, fear, hunger, despair. Humanity has lost its sense of direction, it casts about for the meaning of life and its purpose. (Similarly, the Mayan periods of time have their own characteristics, or 'personalities'.)

These four Yugas represent huge periods of time. The Krita Yuga lasted for 1,728,000 human years, the Treta Yuga for 1,296,000 years, the Dwapar Yuga for 863,000 years, and the Kali Yuga will last for 432,000 years. The diminishing spans of time, and the fact that the Kali Yuga is the shortest, must give rise to hope. Periods are made up of divine years, one year being the lifespan of Brahma. The total, in human years, is 4,319,000. This is equal to 12,000 divine years since any expanse of divine time must be multiplied by 360 to arrive at the number of human years. Each of these universal ages has, like a normal day, a dawn and a dusk, their lengths being one-tenth of the Yuga with which they're associated. While these calculations are currently used by scholars, the great spiritual Hindu, Shri Yukteswar,[19] has calculated that these Yugas are in fact considerably shorter (his methods are based on astrological rather than astronomical cycles).

Despite these different methods, the symbolism and interpretation of the meaning of time remains consistent. The turning of the ages traces spiritual change (on this timescale, it is not overexaggerating to call this spiritual evolution) that parallels physical evolution (*see* Part V) together with the process of degeneration. During these cycles our ability to grasp the meaning of creation, and our place within it, begins with a halcyon, ideal age reminiscent of a vastly more populated Garden of Eden. From this, we decline and fall, and we fall far – from the heights of pristine perfection to the dismal age of a lost humanity. The journey is from supreme spirituality to total materialism where people are concerned only with satisfying their insatiable appetites for things and sensations.

These cycles are never-ending; it's an endless macrocosmic cycle of evolution and degeneration, of the births and deaths of universes which, as with the microcosm of human life, are reincarnated. In the Vedas these cycles of time are called *kalachakra*, the 'wheel of time', and their function is to break up the massive process of creation and recreation into measured periods and movements during which both universe and people can be sustained during identifiable periods. It is for this reason that, in human terms, life and death are illusions. It is only because of time that we are aware of stars being born and of stars dying; it is only because of time that we're aware of birth and the ageing process that carries us to death. For Hinduism, overcoming time is salvation, enlightenment, it is the way to immortality. There are no endings, only new beginnings. Hinduism shares this with the Maya whose prophecies for 2012 are not to be interpreted in terms of gloom and doom. What we face, at the end of each major cycle, is a period of transition, threatening though it may be; where we stand is not on the brink of disaster but on the threshold of a new age.

Buddhism

The Buddhist pattern of time cycling through measureless periods is similar to that of Hinduism. The *mahakalpa*, or Great Aeon, is the largest unit of time. It is measured in millions, even billions of years; we might say it is endless. It is divided into four *kalpas*. A *kalpa* is like a piece of rock a cubic mile in size being rubbed by a ribbon of silk: when the rock has worn away, even one *kalpa* will not be completed. The *vivartakalpa* is the age of evolution during which the universe arises; the *vivartasthayikalpa* is the age of endurance during which the universe is steadily sustained; the *samvartakalpa* is the age of dissolution which sees the demise of the universe; and during the *samvartasthayikalpa* the demise of the universe is sustained in a state of emptiness. It is a period of total annihilation and chaos, when the universe is returned to its original condition. In their turn, each of these *kalpas* is divided into *antarakalpas* of roughly the same length. As with Hinduism, the cycling aeons are divided into periods that plot the creation, demise and recreation of the universe.

For Buddhists, however, time is a function of mind and has no reality of itself. There is only *sunyata*, 'emptiness' or 'voidness'; adjectives that describe the impermanence of all forms and mean that nothing, therefore, has the quality of endurance. We know this to be true of time, something we can't see but can only sense. What is true of time is, for Buddhists, true of all phenomena. Einstein once said, 'If there is any religion that would cope with modern scientific needs, it would be Buddhism.'[22] Had he written specifically about Buddhist concepts of time, he might have discovered that Buddhism is the only tradition that gives us what can be thought of as 'mind-time'. He would also have appreciated and understood that Buddhist meditative practice leads the subject to transcend time, that is, to break free of the mental conventions we use for it.

The Maya

The Maya developed several calendars, and a brief description of the four most important of these now follows.

The Mayan word for 'day' is *kin*, and it is the nearest the Maya get to having a word for 'time'. The *kin* is the basic unit of time. While we are mostly concerned with more extended periods, a very important principle is established by the levels of meaning attached to the term *kin*. Each day has what Tedlock refers to as 'its face'.[24] This is the day's personality or character, and it determines the kind of events that are likely to take place within its duration. What we might think of as our luck or destiny is influenced by 'the face' of, for example, our date of birth. The character and significance of any one day is also related to its two names, its actual name and its divine name, or Day Lord. To this must be added the day's number, which also determines its significance. When a day is referred to or addressed by a diviner, respect for it is shown by giving it the title *ajaw*, which can be translated as 'sir'. Thus, the day Imix would be addressed in this manner: 'Greetings, Sir, Lord 1 Imix.'[24] To underline its importance, the character or 'face' of the day determines the kind of events that might take place on it. While what happens to a person, or what a person decides to do, can be determined by the day's character, the same is true for communities. Thus, some days are better for marriages than others, some for business, and some for specific kinds of agriculture. All the other periods of time, however long, also have a character or personality of their own.

The *tun*, or year, is also the name of the first of the

calendars, one that has probably been in existence since the 6th century BCE. Of all the Mayan calendars, it is the most similar to our own Gregorian calendar. The *tun* year is made up of 18 months (*winals*), each of 20 *kins* (days). Eighteen *winals* amounted to a *tun* of 360 days. To this the Maya add the *wayeb*, a five-day period when the gods withdraw their support. This is not an auspicious period. The full cycle of 365 days (the *tun* year plus the *wayeb*) is called a *haab*. The *tun* year of 360 days starts with the December winter solstice. As with each day of the 20-day cycle, the months also have their own name, number and meaning.

The *tzolk'in*, the second of the calendars, is also based on the 20-day *winal*. This is cycled 13 times, to give a count of 260 days (*see* Table 1). The word *tzolk'in* means 'count of days', and was especially meaningful for the Maya who thought of it not just as a short year, but as a sacred period existing in its own right, and bearing its own significance. The *tzolk'in* is cyclic, in that when the 260 days are completed, they begin all over again. While the *haab* is a civil or secular calendar, the *tzolk'in* is sacred. The relationship between the *winal* (the 20 days) and its 13 cycles is somewhat complex. As Table 1 illustrates, the first 13 of the 20 days are numbered '1–13', with the 14th numbered again as '1', the 15th, as '2' and so on, the last of the 20 days being numbered '7'. For any given day to recur on the same number the full cycle of 260 days must be completed. The names of the days are the same as those of the *tun* month. The meaning of the days of the *tzolk'in* are mostly concerned with agriculture and the cycle of creation, as the table overleaf illustrates.

Unsurprisingly the two significant numbers 13 and 20 have symbolic and mythological associations that apply to the permutations of much longer periods of time. Chac, the god of rain and fertility, is the patron god of the number 13 and Mayan mythology describes 13 heavens and upper levels, while 20 is the number of elemental energies and shares its glyph with the Moon. Together the numbers are associated with specific configurations of powers and forces that influence the unique character of each day of the *tzolk'in*. The 260-day period (20 x 13) is the period required for mountain maize to grow and ripen, it is also, roughly, the 9 months of human gestation. The 260-day *tzolk'in* cycle also represents the cycle of precession (*see* overleaf) which itself, 'represents a 26,000-year cycle of biological unfolding - a type of spiritual gestation and birth - that Earth and its consciousness-endowed life-forms undergo.'[13]

The Calendar Round, the third we need to understand, is constructed by combining and interlocking the *haab* and the *tzolk'in* cycles to produce a new cycle of 52 years. It is a

Table 1: The *tzolk'in* or Sacred Day Calendar Cycle

Winal cycle	Yucatec day names	13-day cycle	Agriculture during the 13-day cycle
1	Imix	1	Sowing
2	Ik	2	
3	Ak'b'al	3	Germination
4	K'an	4	
5	Chikchan	5	Sprouting
6	Kimi	6	
7	Manik	7	Development
8	Lamat	8	
9	Muluc	9	Budding
10	Ok	10	
11	Chuwen	11	Flowering
12	Eb	12	
13	B'en	13	Fruition
14	Ix	1	
15	Men	2	
16	K'ib	3	
17	Kab'an	4	
18	Etz'nab	5	
19	Kawac	6	
20	Ahau	7	
1	Imix	8	
...	...	...	

calendar of great antiquity, and has probably existed throughout Mesoamerica since *c.*2500 BCE. The Chilam Balam of Tizimin wrote, 'This is the Calendar, the summation of the years or Calendar Round. This array of years is continuous to its expected completion ... Then it repeats over and over forever ...'[3]

The Calendar Round combines the 356-day *haab* and the 260-day *tzolk'in* cycle. The solar, or *haab* year of 365 days is cycled 260 times to give a total of 18,980 days or 73 *tzolk'in* cycles. In more familiar terms, it takes 52 years before the first day of the year recurs as the first day of the 260-day cycle. The years themselves are not distinguished by numbering from a certain date as ours are, but the 52-year calendar was adequate for marking specific days and months, or other periods of time, for people to identify dates, events and rituals during the course of a lifetime. One important feature of the Calendar Round was that its termination was believed, like the 5-day *wayeb*, to be a threatening period of unrest and darkness, when the gods withdrew their services. So threatening was the closure of the 52-year cycle that the Maya could not be sure if the gods would allow them another. To ensure this, certain rituals (such as the New Fire Ceremony) were observed, new levels were added to pyramids, or new inscriptions were carved on monuments and steles.

Before we consider the Long Count calendar, it might be useful to summarize the calendric building blocks outlined above.

> The *tun* is made up of 18 months of 20 days each, creating a 'vague', or 'wandering year of 360 days.
>
> The *haab* is a 365-day solar year divided into the eighteen 20-day months of the *tun* with an additional short 5-day month called the *wayeb*.
>
> The *tzolk'in* is a period of 20 days cycled 13 times, giving a 260-day period for the completed cycle.
>
> The Calendar Round is a combination of the *haab* and the *tzolk'in*. When the cycle is completed, it amounts to a period of 18,980 days, or 52 years.

The Long Count calendar, the fourth of the principal calendars, requires more building blocks to be put in place. These are i) the *katun* which is a period of 20 *tuns*, and ii) the *baktun*, which is a period of 20 *katuns*.

All the units of time we have now considered, and the periods they represent, are set out in the following table.

Table 2: The Long Count calendar's units of time using the Yucatec names

Number of days	The Long Count period	Accumulated time	Number of solar years	*Tuns*
1	1 *kin*	–	–	–
20	20 *kins*	1 *winal*	–	–
360	18 *winals*	1 *tun*	≈ 1	1
7,200	20 *tuns*	1 *katun*	≈ 20	20
144,000	20 *katuns*	1 *baktun*	≈ 395 (394.3)	400

The Long Count calendar, or Great Cycle, is made up of 13 *baktuns*. The present cycle started on 13 August 3114 BCE (this date has been calculated by correlating Mayan dates with those on the Gregorian calendar and working backwards). This Great Cycle ends on 21 December 2012, and on the following day a new cycle of 5,126 years will begin. It follows that we are now in the final *katun* of the current *baktun*. As with the 52-year cycle, the ending of both a *katun* and a *baktun* is deeply significant. Each of these periods has, like the *kin*, its own 'face' or personality which will determine its character. As these greater cycles repeat themselves it can therefore be expected that similar events will take place that are consistent with the attributes associated with it.

Just to complete the picture, the Maya had a calendar based on the cycles and phases of the Moon called the *Tun-Uc*. They had problems coordinating the lunar and solar calendars, that is, the period of the Moon's orbit around the Earth with the Earth's orbit around the Sun. The *Tun-Uc* attempts to do this.

Although no calendar associated with Venus has survived, the planet has a significant place in the Mayan system, and the Maya were able to predict accurately the times when Venus would transit the Sun. One of the few surviving sources, the Dresden Codex, includes tables charting the movement and cycles of Venus. It calls the start-date of the Long Count calendar the 'Birth of Venus', and the *katun* that both opens and closes the current Great Cycle is marked by a transit of Venus. One of the visible signs leading to the galactic synchronization of 21 December 2012, is a transit of Venus across the face of the Sun noted for June of that year.

There are some obvious similarities between the Maya's understanding and measurement of time and those of the other traditions discussed here, which raises the question: how far were the Maya influenced by them?

Despite differences of emphasis, the most obvious parallel is the view that time was cyclic. The Egyptians clearly felt the need to balance the linear with the cyclic view of time, while Hinduism virtually deified time, identifying it with Brahma. Apart from that, it is apparent that one feature of Hinduism's measurement of time provides the closest parallel to an important aspect of the Maya calendric system. The Hindu Kali Yuga is described in a strikingly similar way to the final *baktun* of the Long Count calendar. On the proleptic Julian calendar, the Kali Yuga began at midnight on 18 February 3102 BCE; on the Gregorian calendar, on 23 January 3102. The Long Count calendar, as we have seen, is calculated to have begun on 13 August 3114 BCE. The start-date difference is only 12 years between calendric systems developed at opposite sides of the planet. The Kali Yuga is vastly longer than the Long Count period, lasting for 432,000 years, but the reading of it as a 'dark age', as a period of demise, of spiritual darkness, of a time that threatens and challenges, accords well with the Mayan reading of the character of the current *baktun* and the *katun* that closes it in 2012. They share very similar attributes: both were predicted to be periods of ineffective leadership, their rulers taking little interest in spirituality; they were to be times of extreme anger, jealousy and animosity, and would see an increase in murder and sexual crime; they would be characterized by obsessive materialism, and the planet would be ecologically at risk. These excesses are calculated to begin approximately 5,000 years after the Kali Yuga started in 3102 BCE, the problems gathering momentum exactly as the final Long Count *baktun* moves towards its 2012 termination.

Buddhism, which also worked with cycles of aeons, was taken with the abstract nature of time, so much so that Buddhists understood it to be a construct of the mind. It is interesting that the cultures dealing with a cyclic concept seem less concerned with their history, while for those holding to a linear theory, history is avidly recorded in great detail. This is not to say that Hindu and Buddhist history is of little account to those cultures, it is simply a matter of emphasis, the one reading history as a series of fixed events recorded on a calendar for posterity, the other seeing greater significance in the notion of history repeating itself, over and over again.

With certain similarities in these views of time established, they need to be accounted for, and the question of broader cross-cultural influences must be considered. The Maya were unique among the Mesoamerican peoples in having developed a complete written language, but their art and architecture, even their calendars, while not originating with them, were fully developed by them. Direct influence from Egypt has been suggested, but never established. That both civilizations developed a hieroglyphic language suggests the possibility of influence, or a common proto-language. Even this, however, is highly speculative, and a stronger argument could be made for the hieroglyphs having developed locally from pictograms. It is the common use of pyramid architecture that most clearly suggests direct Egyptian influence, although none has ever been proved. The Mayan pyramids were also used as tombs, but the construction served as a platform to elevate the temples and shrines. The structure is more reminiscent of a ziggurat than a pyramid, as is strikingly illustrated by comparing the temple building at Chichén Itzá with the Ziggurat of Ur in modern-day Iraq. Mention has already been made of the Mayan concept of 13 heavens, themselves associated with the 13 *baktuns* of the Long Count calendar. Although the architectural symbolism will vary from site to site according to its prevailing mythology, the construction of a pyramid with 13 steps, the climbing of which is an enactment of passing through these 13 levels, seems entirely logical. The architectural form embodies the mythology and provides a suitable theatre for performing the rituals. No less is true of the architecture of churches, synagogues and mosques designed to express the theology behind the liturgy. A more speculative theory suggests that the ancestors of the Maya were survivors of Atlantis who had built pyramid-like structures themselves.

Those calling on the Atlantis hypothesis resort to Plato's accounts which can be read in his *Timaeus* and *Critias*. But here we are surely in the realm of mythology. What is certainly clear is that the pyramid, with its broad base, is the simplest solution to the problem of constructing a building that is both tall and completely secure, and pyramid builders throughout the world were probably more influenced by the challenge of gravity than by each other. Without any other evidence of influence from ancient Egypt, it is unlikely that the Maya concept of cyclical time was brought from that region.

We are left with the possibility of an influence from the Far East, not in terms of architecture (although connections in this respect have been mooted[25]) but in terms of concepts of time. There is no evidence to suggest that a close encounter between Hindu priests and Mayan Chilam took place that might account for the similarities between the Kali Yuga and final *baktun* of the Long Count calendar. Comparisons have also been made, to little effect, between Hindu sculpture and that of the Maya. An image in Calleman's book,[12] a sculpture of a Buddha, sitting cross-legged in the lotus position, has a pyramid-shaped Mayan temple drawn over it. It's a nice point, but rather than hinting at a direct influence from Buddhism (which Calleman does not argue) it suggests that sitting in the lotus position for meditation is a very stable posture; and it also indicates that Mayan temple rituals may have been concerned with transcendence. Implausibly, it has been suggested[25] that the influence works the other way, that the Maya influenced the Hindu-Buddhist cultures of South East Asia. It is not difficult to come up with such theories, but for want of proof that real and sustained contact was made, they must remain theoretical.

We can't leave this subject without mentioning the hypothesis that the Maya were influenced by extraterrestrial life, and that it was from aliens that they learned about mathematics, astronomy and the cyclic concept of time. Erich von Däniken's *Chariots of the Gods?*, published in 1968, was the first of several books that proposed the 'astronaut theory'. One of the presumed indicators of this idea is the illustration carved on the cover of the sarcophagus of the Mayan sage-king Pacal Votan. Däniken claimed the image of the king suggests the position of an astronaut lying in the space-capsule at take-off, but this has been widely refuted. In summary, there is no evidence that the Maya were influenced by anything or anyone other than their broader geography and their immediate predecessors. We are left with the beguiling notion of parallel but independent development.

— 6 —

UNDERSTANDING THE TIMES

Some historians would like to know if history has a design, if there is a guiding principle that can be discerned in the social and cultural development of society. Their tools are the abstract notions of purpose, intention and reason, and their mandate is to discover if there is a driving energy that orders our world. 'We may not know where we're going,' they might say, 'but we ought to understand our place in the great scheme of things.' Other historians are primarily interested with the factual details, with documenting as completely as possible what has actually happened. Their tools are specialization, statistics and methodology, and their mandate is to account for the way things are to explain how a chain of events has determined the nature of our society. 'We may not know where we're going,' they might say, 'but we ought to understand where we've come from.' The former may not admit to a cyclic view of time, but they will recognize recurrence as part of an evolving plan; the latter will hold rigorously to a linear view of time that threads events on to it by the process of cause and effect. The idea of cyclic time is ancient, and there are cultures founded on this view that are far older than that of the Maya. The notion of time being linear is biblical, the Jews believing that God was a God of history and time, 'like an ever-rolling stream', the vehicle of his progressive purposes. Following through to Christianity, and later to Islam, it is the view that has dominated Western culture.

For the Maya, as we have seen, the linear view of time was a useful and necessary device understood as part of the circumference of time's cycles. While, like the Hindus, they did not deify time, their central god, Hunab K'u represented the fundamental principles of time and space. The codices also identify him as 'Ajaw' or 'Itzamna', names probably representing different facets of one incorporeal, omnipresent and omnipotent being. Hunab K'u was also the god of movement and measure, and the source of numbers and mathematics. The representation of time and space as a god was an acknowledgement that time was sacred, something beyond the mundane that endowed life with meaning. The Maya, not unlike the Buddhists, understood that these dimensions were not created, or inherently part of nature, but existed in the mind. They therefore arrived at a self-definition which enabled them to understand their place in the universe (*see* Part IV). For the Maya, time was sacred, and this gives special significance to their calendars and prophecies.

Our culture is wholly conditioned by the linear notion of time represented in the Gregorian calendar and its Julian predecessor. Calendars are the maps of time, and linear calendars pinpoint our location in the present where we carry the weight of our history with us. Because of their cyclic nature Mayan calendars map the future as well as the past, marking the recurrence of similar events. It is difficult for the Western mind to adjust to the idea that time is cyclic, and to do so would require a huge perceptual change (*see* prophecy 20). To make this change we need to cultivate new habits of thinking, and replacing the Gregorian calendar with an alternative would provide the necessary framework for doing just this. José Argüelles has pointed out that 'the Gregorian calendar measures the Earth's orbit around the Sun, but it's very haphazard and doesn't give any real measure, so it's not a true solar calendar'.[17] What is true of the calendar is also true of the clock; both are devices for measuring artificial time.

> Everything we know about time is rooted in the clock and the clock isn't a measure of time. A two-dimensional plane divided into 12 equal parts of 30

> degrees each is a measure of space – substituted to be a measure of time. All civilization is governed by this erroneous concept that time is something that's measured by the clock.[17]

Already noted is Argüelles' suggestion that we should adopt the lunar calendar of thirteen 28-day months, giving a year of 364 days. Such a calendar would conform to the natural cycles of the Moon and the Sun; that is, every time the Earth goes round the Sun, the Moon goes round the Earth 13 times. We have also seen how the numbers 13 and 20 combine to make up the 260-day sacred count of the *tzolk'in* and Long Count calendars, but despite the numerical and fractal similarities, Argüelles' idea that the lunar calendar is originally Mayan in conception cannot stand. The Mayans supplemented the *Tun-Uc* (the Mayan Moon calendar) with special hieroglyphs, known today as the lunar series glyphs; they used these to record particular dates on the lunar calendar, the name of the current month and its length as, alternately, 29 or 30 days. They tracked the age of the Moon through its phases, the month itself running from new Moon to new Moon and lasting 29.5 days. The alternation of months of 29 and 30 days must have been a means of coordinating the solar calendar with the Moon's phases, though eventually the Maya abandoned their attempts to mesh the cycles of the Sun with those of the Moon. However, the numbers 13, 20 and 260 carry a significance beyond any suggestion of their relationship to a lunar calendar. As we shall see in Part III, 'Getting it Together', the numbers accurately combine to measure the 26,000 years of the Earth's precession, and its climax in 2012, with what is known as 'galactic synchronization'.

Returning to the 13-month lunar calendar, we can see why it is an entirely natural alternative to the Gregorian calendar. Such a calendar would not demand the radical change of consciousness required for us to think of time as cyclic, but this shift to the lunar cycle of which, in so many ways, we are already aware would be a creative start. It would take us from artificial to natural time, from 'an anarchy of time' to the unity of time, from a world splintered by time-zones and the conflicts of competing civil and religious calendars to a world that shares the same calendar as a paradigm and working model for greater unity and peace. In short, our map of time would change significantly and, by habit, so eventually would our consciousness. If time exists in the mind, then a dysfunctional map of time will have an effect on the mind itself. Is it possible that the artificial and arbitrary calendar which programmes absolutely everything we do is causing friction and tensions by steering us away from a natural and harmonious alternative?

PART III

GETTING IT TOGETHER

Our psyche is set up in accord with the structure of the universe, and what happens in the macrocosm likewise happens in the infinitesimal and most subjective reaches of the psyche.

CG Jung

Time is nature's way of keeping everything from happening at once.

Woody Allen

By sheer genius, by sheer acuity, they got it done.

Popol Vuh

How the Maya came by their extraordinary knowledge of astronomy remains a mystery to us since they left no record of their methods. The Dresden, Madrid and Paris codices contain tables and almanacs recording their naked-eye observations. No hint is given of how they measured the movements of stars and planets of which over 3,000 are visible at any one time and location. One theory put forward suggests that among the measuring techniques used were features of buildings which may have served as sight-lines.

> The astronomer Anthony Aveni and the architect Horst Hartung have determined that the ancient Maya used buildings and doorways and windows within them for astronomical sightings, especially of Venus.[26]

Whole complexes of buildings are thought to have represented the constellations with which they were associated, or to have been aligned with the rising, zenith or setting of the Sun, Moon, Venus or star constellation. There is no astronomy without advanced mathematics and the three points, the rising, zenith and setting, provided the triangle that was one of the basic features of the geometry used in their calculations. The only mathematical system that we can say with certainty was used by the Maya is found in the tables of the Dresden Codex, which employs the base-20 (vigesimal) method adopted for both astronomy and the calendars by the Mayan priests and astronomers.

— 7 —

'A MOST UNIQUE CONJUCTION'

Whatever the mathematical methods used, the calculations derived from them were uncannily accurate. For example, the Maya were able to date the eclipses of the Sun and Moon, and the transits of Venus across the Sun's face. These, and other events, were plotted on the calendars that terminate with the winter equinox on 21 December 2012, when the conjunction known as 'galactic synchronization' will provide the climax of the 26,000 years of precession. What exactly is galactic synchronization and what will happen in the immense spaces around planet Earth on that date? The answer is neatly summarized by the Fernbank Science Centre Planetarium of Emory University, Atlanta: 'Planets such as Mercury, Venus, Mars, Jupiter, Saturn, the Sun, and the new Moon will come into alignment with the Earth in a most unique conjunction.'[27] This precessional alignment will include the plane of the Sun's path, or ecliptic, forming a conjunction with the brightest part of the Milky Way between Scorpio and Sagittarius where the galactic centre is to be found. In short, the Earth and the solar system will come into alignment with each other, and with the centre of the Milky Way.

There are several ideas to be considered.

I.) The Five Suns

The 'round figure', 26,000 years, was divided by the Maya into five periods of approximately 5,126 years (totalling 25,630 or 13 *baktuns*) which they called the 'Five Suns'. Traditionally, each of these 'World Ages', or 'creative cycles', ends in disaster. Working backwards through five 5,126-year cycles from 2012, the periods are:

Fifth Sun	3114 BCE–2012 CE
Fourth Sun	8240 BCE 3114 BCE
Third Sun	13366 BCE–8240 BCE
Second Sun	18492 BCE–13366 BCE
First Sun	23618 BCE–18492 BCE

The mythology recounted in the *Popol Vuh*, known also as *The Book of the Community*, explains how humans were created during the age of the First Sun. Geological records show that at that time the Earth was wrapped by an ice age so extreme that most forms of life would have been threatened. There is no evidence to suggest that the period ended with a huge disaster that annihilated life, but a more local disaster might well have impressed itself upon the minds of ancestors of the Maya whose oral traditions lie behind the myths. Whatever natural disaster occurred, it clearly did not happen on the end date of each World Age; what we're considering here is a process that might well have been extreme as one World Age impinged and imbricated on the next. The close of the First Sun and the overlap into the Second Sun, was marked with extreme climate changes that led to the retreat of the ice and the need for human beings to adapt to environmental change. The close of the second cycle sees the ending of the ice age and disastrous flooding. During the third cycle humans began to settle, and early forms of agriculture began to displace hunter-gathering. There were disasters at this time, such as more flooding and volcanic activity, but they were regional, not global. The Fourth Sun, or World Age, followed a similar pattern: fertile land gave way to deserts, and huge floods occurred but, again, these are likely to have been relatively local events. The opening of the Fifth Sun in 3114 BCE also marked the start date of the Long Count calendar, which will end in 2012. The prophecies of what will occur around the end date clearly point to a new World Age, a turning towards a new Sun. But we also turn towards the first *katun* of the First Sun of another cycle of five Suns, and the 26,000 years of a new precessional sequence.

In Mayan cosmology 21 December 2012 marks the end of the Fifth Sun, so are we to expect some form of disaster? Mythology is often the abstraction of real events, accounts of which become an oral tradition, itself eventually set down in a period greatly distanced from the original events by a culture destined to be the custodian of it. Mythology is like the echo of a memory, an atavistic intuition that holds us to a continuum of meaning which helps to make mystery comprehensible. The Mayan prophecy of the current World Age ending in disaster is founded on such mythologies, but we can suppose that behind them were actual events.

The possibility of catastrophe, local, global or galactic, during the *katuns* wrapped around 2012 will be considered in Part V.

II.) The Milky Way

Central to Mayan cosmology is the creation mythology associated with the Milky Way. Allowing for the difference of latitudes, and that the skies above the Mayan astronomers would have been clear and unpolluted, we can observe a similar skyscape, certainly with regard to the Milky Way. From the northern latitudes it is best seen in the summer on a moonless night, well away from artificial light. It stretches across the horizon of the sky from the north-east to the south-east, a luminous path that passes through a number of constellations. It is seen at its brightest between Scorpio and its galactic centre towards Sagittarius. At this, its central point, the Sun is 26,000 light years away, a figure which resonates with the 26,000 years of precession. Interestingly, the galactic centre is now known to be a supermassive black hole, an intense radio source called Sagittarius A*. The Maya could not have known about this, but it accords well with their concept of the galactic centre being the mouth of a monster, or the entrance to a huge cave.

III.) The Tree of Life

The Maya called the Milky Way the Ceiba Tree, which the Book of Chilam Balam of Chumayel describes as 'the first tree of the world'. It is the Mayan Tree of Life, the source and origin of life itself and was thought of as the Cosmic Mother, and also as a snake with the Pleiades forming the rattle of its tail. The dark track running down the middle of the Milky Way is the 'dark rift', or 'dark road' to the underworld, called Xibalba by the Quiché Maya, whose mythology is recorded in the *Popol Vuh*. It has several mythic identities such as the entrance to a cave or tunnel, the crater of a volcano, the mouth of a monster, or an animal like the jaguar, a cleft in the Cosmic Tree itself, or the birth canal of the Cosmic Mother. The dark womb-like centre is where the December solstice Sun crosses the Milky Way, an image of the sexual union of the First Father with the First Mother. This union, effected every 26,000 years, reinforces the concept of the birth of a new age.

IV.) Renewal

The mythologies represent how the Maya understood the origin of the Earth and of life on it, but to appreciate the significance of this we must remember that they were developed with the understanding that time is circular, rather than linear. The difference is critical. If time is perceived as linear, creation would be understood as a process kicked off at a particular time, during a particular period (albeit one that was immeasurably long) by a Genesis-type event that caused everything to come into being out of nothing, and the universe and life on Earth as evolving progressively towards an ultimate, evolutionary goal. If time is perceived as circular, even though the 'big bang' might have determined the structure of our galaxy, there would have been no 'sudden' start that brought the universe into being out of nothing. Some form of creative impulse would always have been in force, and development in evolutionary terms would be understood as a series of renewals, the recurring genesis, a creative energy to which everything that lives contributes. This process of regeneration is continuous and cyclic, as the Mayan concept of five Suns, or World Ages, illustrates, and it has no single, final goal.

For the Maya, the 2012 galactic synchronization is not just a matter of astronomy. The prophecy lies in their interpretation of the event, coupled with the 'character' of the cycled period of time. The Maya prophesied that the energy of galactic synchronization will trigger other synchronizations vital for overcoming the social, ecological and climatic problems that beset us, and these are explored in prophecies 11–14 (*see* Part I). Running through them is a subtler, more abstract, but very significant form of synchronization that we can think of as harmony, a congruency of parts, both to the whole and to each other, as when we talk of melodic harmony and the harmony of the spheres. For the prophecies, harmonious synchronization concerns personal integration, the accord of families, communities, nations and perhaps, most importantly, that of human beings with nature.

— 8 —

PLAYING THE COSMIC GAME

'The ball game ... was the arena in which life and death, victory and defeat, rebirth and triumph played out their consequence.'[10]

Mayan architecture is, in some ways, a symbolic representation of their cosmology and certain star constellations; it is:

> closely related to the cosmic; temples were built with respect to cosmic events. Archaeo-astronomers are still taking measurements today and are astonished at the ingenuity with which the pyramids and entire cities were built.[28]

One of the buildings central to these ritual complexes is not a pyramid or temple, but a structure called a 'ball court', in which a game was played that acted out the drama of Mayan creation mythology and galactic synchronization. It was not a true sport but a ritual enactment that, like the calendars, illustrated the extent to which cosmology was integrated into everyday life. It might be hoped that a game would bring people together, unite them even in the throes of competition, contending without being contentious. Families and groups of friends have always enjoyed playing games at this level, as a leisure activity. But we know only too well that, just as frequently, games give rise to bitter rivalry, especially those played professionally, the worst excesses often coming from supporters rather than players. The 'will to win' is everything, and this is no less true of games as it is of war itself.

The Game

The Mayan ball game is thought to have been played by Mesoamerican people from at least 3000 BCE, effectively since the start date of the Long Count calendar in 3114 BCE. Ball courts have been excavated across Mesoamerica, but no documents explaining the rules of the game have survived. While they vary in size, all these courts have long, somewhat narrow alleyways (or corridors) between high walls, vertical or sloping, off which the ball could be bounced.

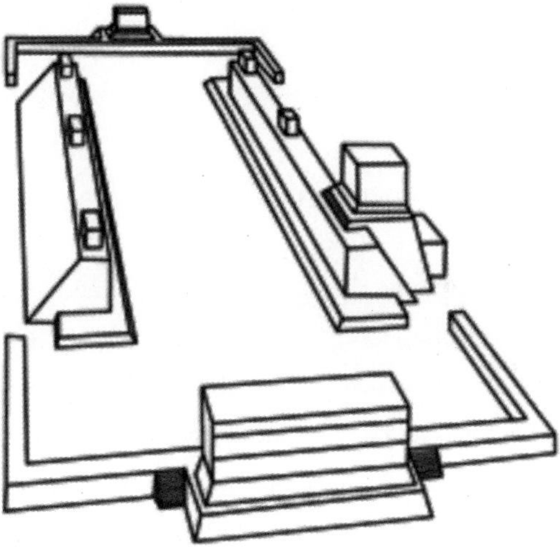

The Ball Court

(based on the Great Ball Court at Chichén Itzá)

Ullamaliztli is the Aztec name for the Mayan ball court, and the game of *ulama*, played in the north-western Mexican state of Sinaloa, is thought to be derived from the ancient game. In the modern game the ground is usually set up temporarily, the opposing teams separated by a line chalked or scraped in the ground. The boundaries are similarly defined and points are won by getting the ball across the 'try' line of the pitch. The game is played between teams of at least five players who compete with a ball made of latex rubber which is some 3kg (6.6lb) in weight. Players strike the ball with their hips, which are protected by specially padded clothing. Another version of the game, in which women can take part, is played on a smaller pitch, with a lighter ball and fewer players, who strike the ball with their padded arms. There is a third version in which the ball is struck with a two-handed wooden panel or racket. The ball has to be kept in play within marked boundaries. [29] Points are gained when the opposing team hits the ball out, or misses the ball, causing it to be 'dead', or strikes the ball out of turn, or touches the ball with the hands or other parts of the body not prescribed, or if a player comes into contact with a team-mate. The game is played to eight points. If there is a draw, the score returns to zero, and the game starts again. Clearly, because of successive draws, the game could go on for a very long time, and there is a record of one that lasted eight days. Most contests are played over two hours even if the game is drawn at 'full time'.

The resemblance between modern *ulama* and the ancient ball court game is slight, but figurines and carved images have been found wearing protective clothing similar to that used by *ulama* players. The construction of the ball court defined the playing area, and ornamented stone hoops attached to the walls suggest that at some point, in some way, the ball would have to pass through them. These hoops, however, are a Post-Classic (that is, post-800 CE) addition. The rule that the ball must remain in play suggests a kind of volleyball without a net, but I know of no other game where the ball must be struck with the hip to keep it in play. In the court at Chichén Itzá, the stone rings were set so far off the playing area that hitting a ball through one must have been such a rare event that, when achieved, probably won the game.

While the rules defining the purpose and structure of the game are lost, numerous sources contribute to our part-understanding of its cultural and symbolic meaning. Such information as we have is drawn from figurines discovered with burials at the sites of ball courts, ceramic ball-game panels, paintings, drawings and carved reliefs such as the one Chichén Itzá. Reliefs at the Zapotec site at Dainzú, show players wearing capes and mask, other murals show men playing in skirts. Generally each player wore a loincloth and protective hip-guards. Depending on the form of the game, they might also have worn garters, girdles, a chest protector, kneepads (in most cases only the right kneepad) and a pad on the right forearm.

The Symbolism

The symbolism of the ball game is complex. Rules, whether applied to a school or a game, are controls to bring order to what otherwise might be anarchy. It is likely that the rules reflected natural laws, for example, those we now call the laws of physics, gravity, motion, and so on, that hold the galaxy in seemingly secure balance. Because the Maya used the game to act out their cosmology there was a great deal at stake both for winners and losers. The 16th–17th-century Franciscan missionary and historian of Spanish colonial Mexico, Fray Juan de Torquemada, records the story of a game being played between Axayacatl, the Aztec emperor, and Xihuitlemoc, the leader of the Xochimilco. The emperor bet his annual income against several of Xihuitlemoc's *chinampas*, 'floating gardens' of richly fertile arable land. Another record[30] tells of Topiltzin, the Toltec king, playing the game against three opponents for the overall rule of the region. This and other similar records offer plausible evidence that the game was played out as a war game to diffuse conflicts caused by rival interests, or inter-tribal war. That the game was an enactment of war is reinforced by illustrative panels in the ball courts showing players dressed in the armour or the uniform of warriors, and bound captives holding the game balls, or 'imprisoned' within the ball itself. More local issues, like boundary conflicts, both in terms of their limits and maintenance, might also have been resolved in the ball courts using the actual limits of the court to symbolize the boundaries in question. It appears that in the larger, more secure states like those of the Aztec, fewer ball courts have been found than in the smaller, less centrally administered states where laws would have been disputed.[30]

The ball game is given another layer of meaning by its astronomical symbolism. In one form of the game the bouncing ball is the symbol of the Sun, and the sacrificial death of a player symbolizes its setting. In this context the game is a conflict between day and night, sunrise and sunset, with the stone rings representing the equinoxes, while the court itself is placed at a key location in the ceremonial complexes. The Maya and other Mesoamerican cultures lived in fear of imbalance in the cosmic order, especially as what was observed in the skies was believed to be paralleled on Earth. The Sun's combat with the 'dark' gods of the underworld during the night illustrates this well. The players are involved in maintaining the balance and movements of the universe, and in the ritual regeneration of its life, the recurrent genesis referred to in chapter 6.

The *Popol Vuh*, the primary source of the Mayan creation

myth, provides the symbolism of the ball game with a mythological dimension. The myth is complex but, put simply, Hun Hunahpú and Vucub Hunahpú (the father and uncle of the Maya hero twins who are central to the *Popol Vuh*'s mythology) were caught playing ball near the entrance to Xibalba, the underworld, whose lords were annoyed at being disturbed by their noise. The head lords, One Death and Seven Death, sent owls to lure the brothers to the ball court of Xibalba itself. When they fell asleep, they were captured, sacrificed and buried beneath the ball court. Hun Hunahpú was decapitated and his head hung in a fruit tree, from where it spat into the hands of a passing goddess who conceived and gave birth to the hero twins, Hunahpu and Xbalanque. Eventually, the hero twins play the ball game against the lords of Xibalba and defeat them. But they never recover their father's body from beneath the ball court, the place of death. Thus, the game can be read as a rite of passage between life and death with the opening to the underworld marked, symbolically, on the court. The overall 'I' shape of the ball court, bounded by the sloping walls, deliberately suggests a sizeable crevice symbolic of the doorway to the underworld. In the *Popol Vuh*, the Quiché Maya word *hom* translates both as 'crevice' and 'ball court', a further confirmation that this aspect of the game was played in deadly earnest as a re-enactment of the *Popol Vuh* drama. The playing of the game also marked the end of cycles of time, such as the end of one world age and the start of another; this remaking of the world associated the game with the creation mythology. It was a game of transition which involved politics, mythology, astronomy and 'the passage of authority from generation to generation through rites of accession'.[31]

The mythic drama of the hero twins is acted out in the glyphs and carvings of the monuments at Izapa which use the story as a metaphor for astronomical events that occur on the horizon towards which the buildings are aligned. Jenkins describes how the ball court on this complex is orientated towards the galactic centre.

> The ... Ball court, orientated to the December solstice horizon, contains thrones and monuments that describe the astronomical convergence occurring in that direction – the convergence of the Milky Way and the solstice.

A Game of Life and Death

Stories are told of the extreme brutality of a game in which the losers were sacrificed to the gods of the underworld, of the 'captain' being decapitated and the head offered as a gift to the gods. The idea is given strength by a skull-rack platform at the Chichén Itzá ball court, the walls of which are carved with rows of skulls, suggesting the use of severed heads as trophies in the game of war.[10] Opinions differ as to the nature and extent of the brutality. On the one hand we have authorities such as Michael Coe telling us:

> The more we learn about the Classic Maya ball game, the more sinister it becomes. In Tikal as elsewhere in the Maya realm, major captives were forced to play a no-win game against the ruler and his team, with eventual loss and preordained human sacrifice as the outcome.[32]

And, on the other hand, Schele and Matthews assure us that 'there is no evidence for this interpretation in any of the ancient or historical sources'.[31] The balance is tipped towards ritual violence by more recent research; Maria Teresa Uriarte is unequivocal in her conclusion: 'The ball game was one means by which human offerings of blood and death were accomplished [offering] the defeated contender in war and conquest the opportunity of being sacrificed with honour.'[33] The evidence includes carved reliefs from several ball game sites; the one at Chichén Itzá, referred to above, shows a winner holding the head of his defeated opponent. It seems, then, that the ball game was literally one of life and death, a violent game played with impunity, in which there was no risk of a player being given a red card for knocking the head off an opponent – always assuming there was a referee. Seen in this way, the game is reminiscent of the Roman gladiatorial games where the luckless losers waited in terror for the emperor's lowered thumb and the death sentence it signalled. Ritually, it is consistent with the Mayan practice of human sacrifice, one that included children and those taken captive in war. With life itself at stake, it is difficult to appreciate that the ball game symbolized the remaking of creation over and over again. The winners must have felt themselves to be like gods, which may well have been the point of it all.

— 9 —

CONJUNCTIONS AND CORRELATIONS

We may think of stars as letters which inscribe themselves at every moment in the sky ... Everything in the world is full of signs ... All events are coordinated ... All things depend on each other; as has been said, 'Everything breathes together.'

Plotinus, quoted by Tarnas[34]

A game may carry symbolic meaning of huge significance, but it remains a game. Life is for real and the Maya were under no illusions – they knew it was 'nasty, brutish and short'. They knew time to be cyclic, but this did nothing to alleviate the problem, in the 16th century, of being an advanced civilization occupied by an invading enemy. Those of us who perceive time as linear can hope that the worst will not last very long; and even if prolonged, it will, eventually, come to an end. We can yearn for the good times to last as long as possible, we can comfort ourselves that the best moments, even if fleeting, will give us a memorable high. The Maya lived with the knowledge that both the worst and the best will recur over and over again, unendingly. The 21 prophecies introduced in Part I confirm that, during the final *katuns* leading to 2012, we are experiencing problems of the kind the Maya lived through when those same *katuns* recurred for them. In receiving the prophecies, we are both cautioned and encouraged; though the threatening events through which the Maya themselves lived are likely to be recycled, encouragement is to be found in the Mayan perception of themselves, that is, of what they would become in our time: custodians and teachers of their wisdom tradition.

The Turning Circles of History

As already pointed out, cyclic time implies cyclic history, and it is the recurrence of events that carries the energy of the Mayan prophecies from their source to our own times. It might be assumed that there is something ideal about a culture that produces prophecy as the first fruit of its spiritual harvest, but such an assumption would be unfounded. The Maya may have spent a great deal of time contemplating the stars, and represented the heavens in their architecture and temple sites, but their society was a long way from being heaven on Earth. Contemporary Mayan elders and shamans are telling the world that they are the custodians of extraordinary wisdom, and are the receivers of a prophetic tradition that anticipated the various crises we are now facing. However, these prophecies do not come to us from a demi-paradise, but from a culture that despite its remarkable astronomy and mathematics, was brutish, violent and cruel, and yet, no more so than our own super-sophisticated and technocratic civilization. If you take a dim view of human nature, you could argue that brutality, violence and cruelty will be endlessly recycled and that the *katuns* and *baktuns* characterized by excessive inhumanity will constantly recycle the horrors of which the human race is capable. We can suppose that the shamans who received the prophecies understood them as warnings to be transmitted, not as stark alarms, but as wisdom appealing for reason and responsible decision in a time of crisis.

It is not only conflict and discord that cycle around; we get the bad with the good. The prophecies place as much emphasis on the urgent need for us to capitalize on and develop our strengths, as on the need to remedy our errors before we get beyond the point of no return. The clear, single message that emerges from the prophecies is that we must redeem the time (*see* Part V). That is, we must transform the character of those *katuns* marked with disaster and negative influences, we must somehow remould them so their characters become creative rather than destructive, their powers synchronized rather than opposed.

The Maya did not prophesy the demise of their own southern city states or the survival of those in the north. This is something of a mystery, since the civilization must have contained the causes of its own decline. This decline happened rapidly during a period of just over a hundred years, roughly 800–925 CE. The dates are marked by the sudden end of the records carved on steles and the cessation of building. It was a time of transition which saw the defeat of rulers in the south, political and territorial changes, large-scale migration, and a new flourishing of the northern states.

While it is curious that there is little record of these events, or of prophecies concerning them, the prophecy of the coming of foreigners, men with beards bringing a new religion, is remarkable. The Chilam Balam of Chumayel tells us that 'Ahau is the beginning of the count, because this was the katun when the foreigners arrived. They came from the east when they arrived. Then Christianity also began...'[4] The period that first brought the Spaniards to the Yucatán was Katun 13 Ahau which ended in 1539. Other prophecies anticipated violence and the deaths of thousands of Mayan people at the hands of the occupying rulers and their missionaries, together with the destruction of most of their codices and wisdom literature.

Those historians with the linear view of time, who say, 'we may not know where we are going, but it is of great importance to understand where we've come from', may not be far wrong. This is especially true of a culture that offers, by means of prophecy, a glimpse into the future state of affairs. History, for the Maya, was not simply an account of past events but an ongoing record of the relationship between prophecy and cyclic time. How we read our history colours our attitude to the present and sets out our priorities for the future. As we shall see, our necessary response to radical change will determine those priorities. By means of the prophecies, Mayan history has been carried into our present. Out of the Post-Classic period of traumatic transition, Mayan prophets anticipated the problems we face in the present day as we move towards 2012 (*see* prophecy 10). The decline of Mayan civilization due to climate change, a reduction of agricultural yield and, most importantly, political strife and the decentralization of authority provided the substance of the prophecies warning us of the threat to our ecology, and of what will happen if we continue to be in opposition to each other and to nature.

Star Signs and Wheels of Fortune

We are born in a given moment in a given place and, like vintage wine, we have the qualities of the year and of the season in which we are born. Astrology does not lay claim to anything more.

CG Jung

Astrology is the interpretation of the synchronicity of the prevailing planetary conjunctions with the date, time and place of a person's birth. It is an ancient art, and as it was used by the Mayan prophets we need to give it some consideration. Astrology provides the individual with a system of self-knowledge that gives insight to the meaning and purpose of a life influenced by the planetary forces of our solar system. Its method is based on what some consider a science: it interprets the significance of the interrelated positions of the planets on the date of a person's birth. That established, a kind of life-trend is indicated, qualified each year during the period of the anniversary of the subject's birth, and each month in association with lunar and other cycles. Specific analysis enables the astrologer to predict a person's future, or at least indicate trends that it may follow. This analysis, which is called a 'horoscope', is an objective record of observable and attestable astronomical data.

In modern astrology, laid over this data is the influence of the so-called '12 houses' representing phases of life or aspects of daily existence. For example, the first house is associated with the development of personality, environment, childhood, and the physical body; the fifth house with procreation, sexuality, pleasure and speculation; the tenth house with vocation, profession and public life.

To these are added the traditional attributes of the signs of the zodiac, each constellation having a dominant or archetypal characteristic. For example, Aries is associated with courage, impetuosity and energy, Cancer with sensitivity, inspiration, creativity and evasiveness, Sagittarius with justice, propriety and sophistry, and Pisces with compassion, tolerance and indolence. The date when the Sun enters each sign is significant; it can be argued that the Sun's relationship with the planets is the most determining factor of a natal horoscope. The ascending and descending axes of the Sun, or its ecliptic, determines the angles of the horoscope to be cast. In broad terms, a new zodiacal sign is on the ascendant every two hours. With the exact date and time of a person's birth and the precise coordinates of the place of birth, the horoscope can be cast. From this information, by means of an ephemeris and complicated calculations (all now available in published tables), the astrologer can determine the auspicious and interrelated zodiacal positions of the planets and the Sun at the place and moment of a person's birth. Further application of the 12 houses is entirely speculative and employs complicated spherical geometry. From a combination of all these factors a person's character can be deduced, together with the kind of life-journey that might be expected.

To take an example, a person born under the sign of the constellation Virgo will be likely to exhibit reason, logic, exactitude and pedantry. At the time and place of the subject's birth, Virgo might have coincided with the third house, the life aspects of which are family relationships and communication. The astrologer will consider the significance of the combined influence of these factors and offer a reading suggested by them. The best readings are not dependent on the data alone, but on the astrologer's intuitive knowledge of astrological symbolism which, in broad terms, can produce a well-pointed account of the person's psychological make-up.

While the Mayan priests offered a divination service and cast individual horoscopes, they were more concerned with the significance of planetary conjunctions for their local communities, and for society as a whole. It can be argued that the Earth itself is a subject for astrological analysis, based not on a birth date, but on the Earth's alignments with other planets at any given time. In interpreting the character of recurring periods of time and transposing that reading into prophecies, the Maya were reading the Earth's horoscope. They seemed to understand that astrology was concerned with archetypes, that is, that behind every form there is an original model, or template, the dynamic of which influences human character and experience. The power of such archetypes goes beyond the matter of mere prediction, and the Mayan Sun-priests were putting together a diagnosis of the Earth based on conjunctions that occur with the solstices and equinoxes across 26,000 years, to the galactic synchronization due in 2012.

The philosopher Richard Tarnas[34] has described correlations he has found between planetary cycles and events on Earth. His is a serious and responsible reading of astrology. It accords well with the Mayan records of correlations of events in their own history with the planetary conjunctions that occurred at the end of each cycle of *baktuns*, and the galactic synchronization marked for 2012. It is not just a matter of conjunction, since opposition is of equal significance. Tarnas is not just concerned with the planetary transits of the galaxy that correspond with those of an individual's birth chart, but with what he calls world transits, 'configurations between two or more planets concurrently aligned with each other in the sky – alignments relevant to the entire world ... rather than to a specific individual'.[34] The cycle he uses is that of Uranus-Pluto, the major alignments of which coincide with radical social and political change such as occurred during the 1960s when the planets were in conjunction, and during the period of the French Revolution when they were in opposition. Tarnas's thesis is a powerful reading of the kind of conjunctions recorded by the Maya. We can only imagine what might happen when the whole galaxy is brought into alignment with the centre of the Milky Way on the winter equinox of 2012.

We owe the concept of the 'axial age' to the German philosopher Karl Jaspers. He used it to describe the period 800–200 BCE, during which dynamic revolutionary thinking occurred simultaneously in China, India and the West. The concept returns us to the idea of parallel but independent development in religion and philosophy during this period: pivotal concepts arose from the thinking of Plato, the Buddha, Confucius, Lao Tzu, Homer, Socrates, and the major Old Testament prophets. Jaspers' concept of an axial age can be applied to other periods, for example, to European movements such as the Reformation of the 16th century and the 18th-century Enlightenment. The 20th and early 21st centuries might well be thought of as an axial age; the devastation of two world wars and the critical changes and challenges characteristic of the period have themselves thrown up extraordinary developments. Science, technology and secularism have taken over from philosophy and religion. The Mayan contribution laid down during their Pre- and Post-Classic periods has confronted us only in recent times, but the combination of their prophecies, founded on mathematics, astronomy and calendric astrology, speaks to us with demanding urgency as we edge towards 2012.

— 10 —

THE MENACES FROM SPACE

Not everything the Maya observed in the skies filled them with joy and wonder. Even today, living in a hyper-rational culture stripped of superstition, we are nevertheless aware of the real threat to the Earth from asteroid impact (*see* Part V). Anthropologists of the future are likely to conclude that 21st-century people have not entirely left mythology behind, nor have we completely let go of our superstitions. Our rites of passage are highly coloured by both, as are our dietary and medical fads. Perhaps it is an odd omission that the Maya left no record of meteorite or asteroid impact, but such near-Earth objects might not always have been visible to the naked eye. Not so comets, to which there are a few references. Fear has an expulsive power; it focuses attention exclusively on its cause, and the absence of reference to other things can be explained by two threats from space with which Mayans lived all the time: Venus and the Moon.

The Morning and Evening Star

The sight of Venus on the Sun is by far the noblest that astronomy can afford.

Edmund Halley

Halley's wonder at the transit of Venus across the face of the Sun is unsurprising. Venus is fixed in the Western mind as the Roman goddess of love, and is associated with romance. After the Moon, Venus is the second strongest light in the night sky, at its brightest just before sunrise and just after sunset, for which reason it is sometimes known as the 'morning and evening star'. The planet's feminine reputation was established early on, figuring in Babylonian texts and mythology *c.*1600 BCE, as the personification of womanhood. The morning and evening appearances of Venus were read by Egyptian and early Greek astronomers as different stars. The Hellenistic Greeks and the Maya knew that it was one and the same star. The femininity of Venus is central to Western astrology, its astronomical symbol being the same as that used for the biological sign of the female sex, a circle with a cross beneath it. Other than the Moon, Venus is our closest neighbour and because, in many ways, it is similar to the Earth, it has been dubbed its sister planet.

The vital statistics of Venus's astronomy seem to confirm its associations with beauty, love and harmony. According to John Martineau, the planet:

> kisses us every 584 days as she passes between us and the Sun ... Venus rotates extremely slowly on her own axis in the opposite direction to most rotations in the solar system. Her day is precisely two-thirds of an Earth year, a musical fifth ... every time Venus and the Earth kiss, Venus does so with the *same face*.[35]

At an average distance of 108.2 million km (67.2 million miles) Venus is the second-closest planet to the Sun. Its journey round the Sun is an almost circular orbit which takes about 225 Earth days, compared to the Earth's orbit of 365 days. It takes a cycle of 584 days for Venus to pass between Earth and the Sun, and it is this passage of the planet across the face of the Sun that is called a 'transit of Venus'. Eight Earth years are equal to 13 Venus years, and every 243 of our years Venus passes between the Earth and the Sun twice in 8 years. For example, two paired transits occurred during the period 1761–9. The first of a paired transit took place 243 years later, on 8 June 2004 and the second will occur 243 years after the 1769 transit, on 6 June 2012. It is interesting to note that these 243-year cycles parallel exactly the number of days it takes the slow-turning Venus to rotate around its own axis, and that during those 243 years, exactly 365 Venus days will have passed. We can, like Martineau, write this off as a solar coincidence, or we can, like Calleman, consider the possibility that:

> this is a type of primal synchronicity which is linked to the fact that Venus has been created as the mirror of the Earth, and maybe in the year 2012, as our consciousness has become more cosmic, this will simply be seen by us as self-explanatory.[12]

Romance, harmony and synchronicity apart, the Maya considered Venus to be a real menace, it was their 'dark planet', the Mayan Mars, and they associated malevolent and violent gods with this morning and evening star. One of the main centres used by the Mayan astronomers was a circular building, the Caracol at Chichén Itzá, an observatory built specifically to record the movements of Venus. The fullest account of the Caracol records is found in the Dresden Codex. Another site, the Nunnery Complex at Uxmal, has 584 windows, matching the number of days in a Venus cycle,[13] the cycles themselves being prescient of drought, danger and warfare. The start date of the Long Count calendar, 13 August 3114 BCE, is referred to as the 'Birth of Venus', and the final *katun* of the last *baktun* of the Long Count sees a pair of transits across the face of the Sun.

The malign influence of Venus was most potent at its heliacal rising and setting (the first visible rising or setting of Venus before or after conjunction with the Sun). Ronald Bonewitz asks:

> Why were particular astronomical conditions seen as so dangerous that they needed the offering of human life to prevent some dreadful occurrence? The answer must lie in some dreadful celestial event in the past, at a time when Venus was prominent to the Maya ... an event that affected many civilizations worldwide ... Few celestial happenings could strike such terror into the hearts of men, but an impact of a comet or its fragments is certainly one of them.[36]

Whatever the nature of the catastrophe that determined the Mayan view of Venus, the fear ran deep and was part of the mythic consciousness they inherited from earlier local superstitions. When the planet rose, people closed their doors and windows against its malevolent light, believing it to be the carrier of ill fortune and sickness. The worst days, when all of nature would be threatened, was when the planet rose after an inferior conjunction. The image used is of Venus as a hurled spear and the Dresden Codex lists the spear's targets on specific days, such as the aged, the lords, the young, rain and the lack of it, resulting in drought.

The position of Venus was used to find the most auspicious date for opening a military campaign and inscriptions record that the evening rising of Venus was the signal for an attack. Local wars increased in frequency during the 8th century CE, the fiercest in Mayan history, the captives being used for human sacrifice. As the sight of Venus signalled the start of a battle, the practice of sacrifice would also have been associated with the planet. The higher the ranks of the captives the more efficacious the sacrifice. One prisoner, a ruler called Siebal, was kept alive for 12 years in order to be offered in sacrifice at a certain conjunction with Venus.[36] The planet was also believed to be a personification of Kukulcan or Gukumatz (a deity known to the Aztecs as Quetzalcoatl). Each of the three names translate as the 'feathered serpent' or the 'plumed serpent', and are associated with wind and war. In the mythology, Kukulcan had sacrificed himself by plunging into fire, as Venus seems to do when it transits the Sun. Belief in the return of Kukulcan, figured in the cycles of Venus, was central to the cult that spread throughout Mesoamerica. The mythology ran so deep that in November 1519, Montezuma II, the ruler of the Aztecs, believed the Spanish conquistador Hernán Cortés to be either an emissary of Kukulcan, or the god himself. He greeted Cortés with the words, 'My royal ancestors have said that you would come to visit your city and that you would sit upon your mat and chair when you returned.'[4]

The belief in Kukulcan's return lies behind prophecies 2 and 4, which imply that the return of the god will not be actual, but manifest in people themselves, aspiring to the spiritual attributes of the supreme being through their own spiritual evolution.

Venus is the only major planet to revolve in a contrary direction, and this might have contributed to the Maya sensing its malevolence. The extreme threat the planet appears to pose is cushioned by its more positive associations with the return of the god Kukulcan at a time when we have the greatest need, however that return is interpreted.

The Vile Thing of the Night

This is the flower of the night ...
a star in the sky.

This is the vile thing of the night: it is the Moon.

The Book of Chilam Balam of Chumayel

The Maya were the only culture in Mesoamerica to have a calendar dedicated, exclusively, to the Moon. Reference has already been made to this calendar, known as the *Tun-Uc*, '*tun*' meaning 'count' and '*uc*' meaning both 'Moon' and 'seven'. Why 'seven' is unclear, unless it is a gloss by a translator, referring to the seven-day week of the Gregorian calendar.

The astronomers aimed to give some fixed form to what they felt was an erratic lunar year, and they used the lunar series glyphs mentioned in chapter 6 to do so. This erraticism is one of the reasons why they were disenchanted with our closest planetary neighbour. Their irritation is expressed by the Chilam Balam of Tizimin who noted, 'Yaxum our forefather cast aside the divisions of the katun pertaining to the Moon.'[5] ('*Katun*' is probably best read here as 'calendar'.)

For this reason the Maya kept separate records of the Sun's movements and the Moon's irregular phases. The period of the synodic (lunar) month was calculated from new Moon to new Moon, an average of 29.5 days, but the Mayan astronomers recorded alternate months of 29 and 30 days in an attempt to coordinate the Moon's phases with their calendar. By this means they knew its age in days on any specific day of the month, and where it came into conjunction with Venus. The phase of the Moon on any given day is interrelated with the *tzolk'in*, where both images and texts describe the 'burden' of the Moon goddess on that particular day (that is, the influence of the Moon on the 'character' of the day). The Moon also imposes on the day the activities associated with the goddess, such as medicine, childbirth and weaving. In practical terms, therefore, the Moon touches the daily lives of the villagers.

The Mayas' fear of the menacing Moon was caused, in part, by the difficulty they had in recording its phases with the same meticulous order given to their observation of Venus and other planets. The Moon was moody and unpredictable, and it had a dark side. In the Book of Chilam Balam of Chumayel, there is a reference to the disastrous Katun 11 Ahau:

> When the invasion came during Katun 11 Ahau, even the Heavens pitied themselves. They blamed it on the Moon when our warriors cut their own throats.[4]

There are other references to the Moon's influence on rain, and as the cause of flooding; still others associate it with drunkenness, lust and sinful love. There are ominous Moon-related readings for Katun 13 Ahau, and the prophecy warning of a new religion which, once enforced, will determine that:

> there is no lucky day for us. It is the cause of death from bad blood [probably dysentery] when the

> Moon rises, when the Moon sets, the entire Moon, this was its power; it was all blood.[4]

Prophecy 8, in the summary given in Part I, concerns the cycles of the Moon's phases in the final *katun* ending in 2012, and it is less than positive. The Moon's own character of deceitfulness, promiscuity and unpredictability suggests events that will challenge mankind. Flooding has already been cited, as has drunkenness, but in this context it implies humanity's unrestrained behaviour, and its intoxication with materialism. On the other hand, the Moon's connection to childbirth is a reminder of the rebirth of a more vital consciousness, wisdom and cosmic awareness.

The extremes are clear, the outcome, like the vagaries of the Moon itself, is in the balance.

PART IV

WHO ON EARTH ARE WE?

In lak'ch (I am another you)

A Mayan greeting

What a piece of work is a man, how noble in reason, how infinite in faculties, in form and moving how express and admirable, in action how like an angel, in apprehension how like a god! the beauty of the world, the paragon of animals...'

Shakespeare, *Hamlet*

The series of prophecies given to us by the Maya all lead to the daunting conclusion of prophecy 21, that we – the people alive in the years leading up to 2012 – are the prophecy. By trick of birth, because we happen to be living now, we are the people of the time when the Mayan Long Count calendar reaches its end date. In short, the buck stops with us. We will witness galactic synchronization and live through the first years of the new cycle of precession, but can we hope that the generations living around the 2012 end-date will, at least, see the beginnings of the prophecies' fulfilment? What distinguishes us as the extraordinarily timed recipients of these prophecies? How did the Maya understand themselves, and what did they make of human life in particular?

— 11 —

CREATION AND ITS MYTHS

The origins of life are obscure, but a persistent curiosity drives the human species to account for its beginnings. The bicentenary of the birth of Charles Darwin in 2009 generated great interest in the theory of evolution. Darwin's theory explains how a process of gradual biological change has given rise to the variety of life forms on Earth. Evolution, however, does not address the question of when and where life started. Ever since human beings have formed communities, either as hunter-gatherers or settlers, this pressing and basic question has thrown up all manner of creation myths. Every religion, every culture, has developed a creation myth that accounts for the origin of the universe and life within it.

Most familiar to westerners is the account given in the Book of Genesis. This has been displaced by modern scientific theories of the origins of the universe and of life on Earth, but the question as to where life itself came from remains unanswered. Many theories have been put forward, such as spontaneous generation, abiogenesis, autocatalysis, clay theory and the possibility that life had its origins not on the surface of the Earth, but several miles below it. From the 'deep-hot biosphere' within the Earth it is, for technology and science, only a short step to the suggestion now being put forward of exogenesis, the belief that the origins of life are extraterrestrial. Panspermia, one possible form of exogenesis, is the notion that the seeds of life are scattered throughout the universe. Don Isidro, a contemporary Mayan shaman, tells us:

> It is certainly interesting to know we come from the stars, but even more interesting is the realization that we're part of the cosmos. Although we might be only a spark in the immensity of the universe, we are the Great Father's children and our destiny is linked to that of creation.[37]

The Mayan creation myth told in the *Popol Vuh* is multi-layered and complex and is worth looking at more closely. It offers an interesting commentary on how the Maya understood themselves as people, and provides insights into the nature of some of the Mayan prophecies for 2012.

The *Popol Vuh*, a book predating the Spanish conquest, is now the principal source of the Quiché Maya creation myth.

Like all ancient religious literature there are several sources behind the version we now have, one of which was referred to by its authors as an *ilb'al*, an 'instrument of sight or vision'.[37] It describes how the gods created human beings out of basic raw materials:

> And here is the beginning of the conception of humans, and of the search for the ingredients of the human body ... And these were the ingredients for the flesh of the human work, the human design, and the water was for the blood. It became human blood, and corn was also used by the Bearer, Begetter ... the making, the modelling of our first mother-father, with yellow corn, white corn alone for the flesh, food alone for the human legs and arms ...[37]

The description of the use of raw materials is reminiscent of the creation myth of Genesis, in which God models Adam out of dust (Genesis 2:7). And like the Creator of the Old Testament, the gods in the *Popol Vuh* did not get it right the first time, in fact they had to make several attempts, first modelling humanity out of mud and wood before deciding on maize (corn). This final choice is perhaps unsurprising since maize was the staple diet of the region, the cultivation of which dominated Mayan agriculture. As we shall see, the crop had considerable symbolic value.

When they 'awakened to the light', the first human beings were filled with gratitude and thanked the Bearer, Begetter for giving them mouths, faces and the ability to speak and listen, to wonder and move; and they thanked him for knowledge and understanding. The myth explains that these proto-humans were omniscient, and on the assumption that knowing all things leads, if not to omnipresence, then to omnipotence, the gods, in fear of a challenge to their own status, decided to adjust their handiwork. This they did by setting a limit to the kind of knowledge with which the first people had been endowed. This also resonates with the Genesis myth, in which all human suffering is due to Adam and Eve's eating the fruit of the tree of knowledge of good and evil. For the Maya, the quest is to regain the knowledge withdrawn by the Bearer, Begetter, a quest realized in part by the prophecies given to the Chilam. Regaining this 'original', or pristine knowledge is the basis of prophecies 12 and 14, which speak of a new enlightenment and recovered memory. The idea that we only have partial knowledge is an important theme, and it will be considered later.

The *Popol Vuh* lists what the Maya understood to be the most important characteristics of being human:

> They were good people, handsome, with looks of the male kind. Thoughts came into existence, and they gazed; their vision came all at once. Perfectly they saw, perfectly they knew everything under the sky, whenever they looked ... As they looked, their knowledge became intense ... They talked and they made words, they looked and they listened. They walked and they worked.[37]

To understand the weight of this mythology and how it applies to the prophecies, we need to look at these discerning characteristics.

Doing the Right Thing

'They were good people' is the characteristic that leads in the *Popol Vuh* creation myth. Among the many books written about the Maya few, if any, are concerned with morality and ethics. It is not an easy subject to consider. We have, on the one hand, prophecies concerned with the transmission of knowledge, with masters and teachers, with a transition to a 'New Age', with enlightenment and cosmic consciousness and, on the other hand, a culture that is critically flawed by cruelty, bitter wars and human sacrifice. It seems that great wisdom walked hand in hand with inhumanity. Such extremes can't be reconciled, and the prophecies that speak of the need for us to face our own shortcomings, and the problems caused by them, in no way mitigate the atrocities perpetrated by the Maya. At the very least, we must listen to those prophecies, if for no other reason than to learn from their experience.

The mores of one society are sometimes the taboos of another. The Maya of the Classic period deformed the heads of their babies so that their foreheads sloped steeply. It seems the cause for simulating this simian effect was the Mayan interest in snakes, and the belief that the shape mimicked the appearance of an earlier, aristocratic, proto-Mayan ancestry. As did other peoples, the Maya filed their teeth, tattooed and scarified their bodies for the purpose of decoration, or in the practice of rituals. Excessively brutal forms of child sacrifice, incomprehensible to modern-day westerners took place. The best we can do is to consider this in its own context, that is, within the Mayan world view. We do not see the world through Mayan eyes, we do not live with their political or agricultural problems, we are not under the authority of their religion and its complex pantheon of contending gods. We have sophisticated philosophies, complex administrations, a developed system of education and healthcare, and hugely advanced science and technology that provide answers to questions that were, for the Maya, mysteries wrapped in fear rationalized by myths and superstitions. The Mayan numerical system, mathematics and astronomy were developed alongside an elaborate animism; this remains an anthropological conundrum.

However these contradictions arose, human sacrifice was a vital and sustaining aspect of Mayan cosmology and way of life. The *Popol Vuh* tells of the gods creating the human race as a source from which they would be supplied with nourishment in the form of human sacrifice, the offering of which was an acted parable of prayer. A further explanation, one we have already discussed, is that Venus was identified with a disaster of such terrifying menace that only human sacrifice could prevent its recurrence. The New Fire ceremony was one of the principal ceremonies centred on ritual sacrifice, practised to initiate a new Calendar Round, or as a termination ceremony held on the last month of the year. At such a time:

> the priests watched the movement of the stars we call the Pleiades ... if they passed overhead at midnight, then the fire priests proceeded; they ripped out the heart of a sacrificial victim ... and started a flame with a fire drill in his open chest cavity.[38]

Life for the Maya was brutish and risky; their world view, therefore, concentrated on the forces that were life-giving and life-threatening. Sacrifice, whether of animals or human beings, takes many forms but all of them symbolize the offering of the self. Put simply, humans were sacrificed to the gods as reimbursement for the gift of life.

It is tempting to rationalize the barbarity of Mayan practice as that of a primitive people, but, as we have seen, they were not primitive. In their time they established a sophisticated civilization, being the only Mesoamerican culture to develop a form of writing, based on a hieroglyphic alphabet of something like 850 characters, which we can still see carved on steles, monuments and temples, on jade, wood and shells and in the surviving codices. Mayan architecture was as remarkable as that of ancient Egypt, and mathematics, astronomy and calendars were highly developed. What it seemed necessary for them to do would be deemed by us to be inhuman and unlawful, but we must beware of making value judgements. In recent history the world has been riven by two world wars, the holocaust, terrorism and numerous other wars, all of which debase the quality of what it means to be human every bit as much as did the Maya's practice of sacrifice. Modern-day man has threatened the survival of thousands of species of plants, animals and fish. Westerners live in relative comfort while hundreds of thousands of people living in less fortunate regions suffer drought and famine, and die of starvation or preventable diseases. Are we more civilized than the Maya?

The prophecies warn us of the superficiality and vulnerability of our civilization. Stripped of the technology and science that furnish and secure the comfortable accoutrements of our life, society would rapidly descend into barbarity – a concept powerfully illustrated in fiction, such as William Golding's *Lord of the Flies*, Cormac McCarthy's *The Road*, and post-catastrophe television dramas such as *Survivors*. If we were pressed to survive in a threatening environment, among threatening groups competing for whatever natural resources were left, our standards of what 'doing the right thing' means might well be revised. In such a context the survival of the fittest takes on a whole new dimension, there is no absolute ethic, and morality becomes relative to people's needs and circumstances. For countless animals and plants the struggle to survive has already reached the point of no return, while in many places in the world human life has been reduced to a scrabble to subsist. The prophecies warn that the numbers at risk will increase alarmingly.

One of the remarkable things about the prophecies is that they anticipated the causes of what threatens us; another is that they focus with disarming accuracy on what we must do to redress the situation.

Thinking the Right Thing

In the *Popol Vuh* myth, the faculty of thought came early in the creation process: directly after their bodies were described, 'thoughts came into existence'. Thought is a function of the mind, and the mind a faculty of the brain. The ability to think conceptually, to reason logically and to make connections between seemingly incongruous ideas and events is one of the characteristics that distinguishes humans from other animals. Once people are endowed with the ability to think, it is possible for everything else to fall into place.

It is impossible to enter the mind of the Pre- and Post-Classic Maya, even with the help of contemporary teachers and shamans. In the highlands of Guatemala where the traditions have survived, the *tzolk'in* diviners can be seen at work and consulted; a visitor can even undergo a form of initiation. But time and the influence of the modern world will have had an effect on the received oral and written traditions, distancing the concepts and practices from original thought and perceptions even as, for example, in the West no established form of Christianity reflects the concept of the faith envisaged by Jesus and the Early Church. Everything evolves, even the most sacred and fundamentalist ideas. The German philosopher Ludwig Feuerbach famously said, 'Man is what he eats.' So much for the body; of greater significance is the teaching given in the *Dhammapada*, attributed to the Buddha, for whom the mind was everything: 'All that we are is the result of what we have thought: it is founded on our thoughts, it is made up of our thoughts.'[39] This truth lies behind prophecies 12 and 13; both are concerned with the quality of mind, and with the kinds of thought it entertains.

The prophecies tell us that in the years leading to 2012 and beyond, the human species, if it is to survive, will need to develop a broader mind and fuller, more sweeping perceptions. 'Cosmic consciousness' is a term used by both Eastern and Western mystics and by ancient and New Age religions. The cultural historian Piero Scaruffi has made the perceptive suggestion that the mental is a property of matter.[40] It echoes the Mayan notion, which lies at the heart of all their teachings, that the entire observable universe is energy, an idea supported by modern physics. That being so, what we term 'cosmic consciousness' is not something born of mysticism, and referring to the cosmos is not, in fact, 'other worldly'. Cosmic consciousness is being aware that we are an integral part of everything, however distant, however close.

In the West, with its entrenched tradition of dualistic philosophy, this kind of concept is dismissed as a product of intellect, an impractical idea so heavenly minded that it is of no earthly use. And that is the problem: if the idea of cosmic consciousness remains just that, an idea, a merely intellectual notion, it will achieve nothing. What the prophecy is concerned with is consciousness as *experience*, not as idea. The experience of oneness is something to which all religions aspire; Hindus and Buddhists are very familiar with it, those who hold to the biblical religions less so. For them, the experience of 'oneness' is an attribute of mysticism to which only a minority have access. For the Maya, cosmic consciousness was not a refined form of spirituality but a birthright, the inheriting of which is aided by a form of initiation, such as the 'solar initiation' led by the contemporary Mayan elder Hunbatz Men in 1995. The idea is close to that of Buddhist enlightenment, in that the initiate will be awakened as if from sleep. It is the subject of prophecy 12. Such a concept was, for the Maya, woven into the fabric of everyday life, since the 'idea' was translated into experience. William James put it this way:

> Our normal waking consciousness, rational consciousness as we call it, is but one special type of consciousness, whilst all about it, parted from it by the filmiest of screens, there lie potential forms of consciousness entirely different ... No account of the universe in its totality can be final which leaves these other forms of consciousness quite disregarded.[41]

The period of transition through which we are now passing, leading to galactic synchronization, will move us from an age of belief to an age of knowledge. Belief is a matter of faith, of accepting for whatever reason that something is true or reliable. We are likely to *believe* that a doctor can help us, even if we're meeting the doctor for the first time. Belief is founded on trust which may, or may not, be based in experience. On the other hand we *know* the Sun will rise tomorrow, a claim that in terms of probability theory is incontestable. The prophecy of a new enlightenment is of our transition to this kind of certainty. The Chilam Balam of Tizimin assures us that we 'will begin to esteem our learning and our knowledge of the unrolling of the face of the universe'.[5]

Saying the Right Thing

The *Popol Vuh* creation agenda continues with the gifts of speech, observation and reflection: 'They talked and made words. They looked and they listened.' While communication, by one form or another, is a facility we share with all forms of animal life, only human beings can speak, and the Mayan myth highlights language as a pivotal human characteristic. Speech, as used by humans is a particular form of language, complex, subtle and capable of an almost unlimited range and nuance of meaning across something like 6,912 living languages. The Mayan vocabulary developed to include signs and symbols found throughout the whole of nature; everything was there to be read, from the most distant stars observable to the naked eye, to the details of landscape, flora and fauna.

The account of creation given in the Prologue of the first chapter of St John's Gospel not only places language at the centre of the creation process, but identifies the 'Word' with God, and describes it as the means or mechanism of creation, 'When all things began, the Word already was. The Word dwelt with God, and what God was, the Word was ... and through him all things came to be: no single thing was created without him.'[42] The *Popol Vuh* offers a similar account, describing how the Bearer, Begetter first talked, then thought and worried about creation, following which, 'they agreed with each other, they joined their words, their thoughts, and then it was clear'.[43]

There is huge power and energy to be found in the 'Word', and in whatever sign or symbol assumes the same role. It is extraordinary that what is merely a sound can be identified with a specific meaning; it is even more remarkable that across all the languages of the world, the range of these sounds is so extensive as to be virtually infinite. Little wonder that the Maya knew language to be a miraculous gift, and understood speech to be the medium of creation and their most direct link with the gods who created. Because they read everything in nature as a message-carrying sign, they understood that behind the pantheon of gods and the plurality of creation was an underlying and dynamic unity. We have already seen how the Maya understood that the Earth, the life dependent on it and the whole observable universe was sustained by a single energy. This unifying energy is embedded in the creation myth, in which the Bearer, Begetter 'agreed with each other'. There could have been no creation out of discord, only out of harmony, and it is this same enlightened perception that lies behind prophecy 11, the urgent call to realize the unity inherent in mankind. That the creating gods were in tune with each other is a figure of our need to be in tune with the universe they created. Who can tell what humanity might achieve if it were to work out of this kind of harmony?

The myth continues: 'They looked and they listened.' Speaking complements listening; both complement observing. 'You listen but you do not hear, you look but you do not see', is an admonishment given by many religions, teachers and parents. The Mayans' astronomy is the greatest testimony to their powers of observation; the phenomena they recorded were observed with the naked eye over long periods of time. To observe closely and intelligently is a form of focused consciousness: looking makes us aware of things and it is revelatory, as anyone who has attempted to draw from life will affirm. If you attempt to draw a tree or a building, however poor or good the result, you will see things you have never seen before and your perception of the subject will change.

We know what the Maya saw in the stars. Their observations were recorded in the tables of their codices, constructed in stone on their temple sites, organized in their calendars and communicated through the prophecies given by the Chilam. Naturally, we don't 'hear' the prophecies, we don't listen to them as did the ancient scribes, and unless we learn to read the hieroglyphics, our access is through the translations made of them. If the prophecies speak to us, then we can only listen with our minds. It is all about words and what we do with them; it is language that carries our quest, but it is intuition that enables the crucial leap from idea to experience. This is what the Maya prophesied would happen, and why one of the leading prophecies, prophecy 2, is about the emergence of a new generation of masters and teachers, born in our time to deliver the Mayan message directly. It could be argued that what I am writing now is a part-fulfilment of the prophecies that point to a gathering interest in the Mayan message during the years leading to 2012.

Following the gift of thought, language is the most distinctive human characteristic. Indeed, thought and language go together; we cannot have one without the other. Communication by words, spoken or written, carries its own problems and its own responsibilities. When we speak or write we may fail to represent clearly our own intended meaning, or the meaning of the source we want to share; this can take the form of deliberate misrepresentation as happened when the Catholic priests accompanying the Spanish conquistadors rewrote some of the Mayan codices with a Christian interpretation. When we listen to what others say we can be caused to think in ways that have never before occurred to us. This can be part of the natural process of learning, or the influence of subversive teaching. The prophecies are the communication of truths of which successive generations of Mayan elders have been custodians; listening to them, reflecting on them is, as prophecy 14 suggests, like recovering a memory.

The words of the prophecies help us to regain a pristine truth, a perception of things as they were intended to be. In recovering the words, it is hoped we might also recover the state of being that was originally intended for us.

The Community of the Universe

The combined characteristics of being human, set out in the *Popol Vuh* creation myth, do not add up to what it means to be a person. For the Maya, personality and individuality are best understood by what the myth has to say about community. The Maya's paramount concern was the role of the individual in society. This, in turn, made the ideal of unity a basic value.

The *Popol Vuh* myth does not suggest that there is an ultimate or ideal template on which the individual was patterned, as does, for example, the Genesis myth which asserts that each person is created in the image of God. In Mayan society, the individual (and individuality) was subservient to the community; personal interest gave way to the common good. Rather than a picture of society being a grouping of individuals with personal autonomy, we are given an image of interdependency. For the Maya, the notion of community included everything created: each separate entity of the observable universe and immediate environment contributes its indispensable part to the whole. Jean Molesky-Poz, quoting Thorn, offers a fascinating account of how the maize (corn) from which humans were modelled, became a symbol of group identity. (The image is of the whole cob in relation to its separate kernels.)

> Corn is what gives meaning to ethnic identity and to a cultural universe. Corn has a 'mythic' value, not a commercial one. Corn is an emblem for the Mayan community. Individual kernels are of no consequence as such.[44]

Corn, as the staple diet of Mesoamerica, is no more surprising an emblem of a people and its culture than, for example, English roast beef or American apple pie. The ideas the food conjures allows it to become a symbol of cultural associations and national characteristics.

The message of the prophecies combine to warn us that unless we overcome the differences that cause strife, tension and war, our civilization will be at serious risk. The vision of unity lying behind Prophecy 11, is given by the Chilam Balam of Tizimin: 'I say the divisions of the Earth shall be one!'[4] A further prophecy is given by Pacal Votan: 'I come to you as the special witness of time to remind you, especially on the day of truth, that in your origin you are one, and on the day of truth you are to make yourselves one again.'[7] There is nothing original in the Mayan vision of unity, it is the heart of the teachings of most of the world's major religions, which, since their foundation, have exhorted their followers to 'hang together'. The tragic irony of history is that the passion to preserve unity has become one of the most divisive energies. Nor are the Maya alone in warning us, by their own example, of the need to overcome differences in order to avoid bitter internal conflict. They have another hard lesson to offer: true unity cannot be imposed, whether by centralized control or government, or by an occupying enemy.

Among the prophecies that speak of the increase of even greater threats to our ecology and climate (prophecy 16), of changes to the Earth's magnetic field (prophecy 17), of the need to transcend our technology (prophecy 19), the prophecy of realizing an underlying unity is the most hopeful and positive. It suggests that as the things of the world break up, the things of the spirit, or higher consciousness, will gather together. Is this just wishful thinking? So much in early 21st-century society seems to be working against any chance we may have of unity. Mankind is riven by differences in political and religious ideologies, by cultural and racial conflict, by the gap between the rich and the poor, by inequality in a class system that is still very much part of our lives and which, itself, is caught in the tension between privilege and meritocracy. Since the end of the First World War there have been many initiatives bent on making the implicit unity of the human race actual. The unity of which the prophecy speaks has a far broader concern than alleviating political, social and religious difference. Behind the more overt movements for reconciliation and partnership, such as the Ecumenical Movement and the European Community, lies an ancient but ever vital energy, as pointed out by Carl Johan Calleman:

> The most advanced ancient and spiritual traditions of the West and East, the Mayan and Vedic, have been unified in a common framework for understanding the future of humanity.[12]

This positive theme is shared by Paramahansa Yogananda: 'All the world's great religions are based on common universal truths, which reinforce rather than conflict with one another.'[45] Such thinking is an indication that the prophecy of unity is, at least, generating the energy for its fulfilment. The World's Parliament of Religions had its first meeting in 1893, and the mission statement of the modern-day Council for a Parliament of World Religions might well be the mandate of this Mayan prophecy, its aim being 'to cultivate harmony among the world's religious and spiritual communities and foster their engagement with the world and its other guiding institutions in order to achieve a just, peaceful and sustainable world'.[46] Other movements for unity and reconciliation include Lord Carey's (the previous Archbishop of Canterbury) InterFaith Initiative which endeavours to focus on the essential truths and common quests shared by most religions, and the Mayan initiative led in 1995 by the contemporary elder Hunbatz Men at the temple site of Chichén Itzá. This event was attended by Tibetan lamas and the Wisdom Conservancy, whose mission statement explains:

> Via modern means we conserve the life wisdom of learned and compassionate people from around the world. TWC uses this resource to develop educational programs, books, videos and other media. We support and encourage the public in cultivating and applying wisdom to help establish a more just and enduring civilization.[47]

The ideal, the ultimate way of being, is the coming together of all the parts to work in unison. For the Maya, the model of what people should strive for in society was the harmony of uncountable elements of the universe sustained by physical laws that hold everything in balance. The prophecies warning of the disasters gathering towards the winter equinox of 2012 are all founded on the problems caused by our society failing to achieve the kind of working harmony visible in the night skies.

Generally, people would agree that unity is desirable, but few have lived with it for any length of time. The Maya themselves were not a unified people. They existed in something like 20 separate, independent states bound by a common culture spread across Guatemala, the Yucatán and southern Mexico. In addition to inter-state conflict, tension was caused by a strict class system centred on a hereditary absolute monarchy. This, in turn, was served by provincial governors and an educated middle class of administrators, scribes, priests, architects, etc., and by the labouring and farming community. If the Maya knew what it was to live at peace among themselves, or with their neighbours, it can only have been for short interludes during the Classic period (*c.*250–800). They, like us, would have discovered that a common enemy, or widespread natural catastrophe, are strong forces for social cohesion. And they too must have yearned to be at one with themselves, with each other and with nature. The phoenix that rose from the ruins of Mayan civilization is not the hope of a future paradise where 'the wolf will lie down with the lamb' (Isaiah 11:6), where everything and everyone will live in unbroken peace. Instead, the vision is pragmatic, it is of a functional society that, rather than using its resources and energies to resolve conflict, combines to resolve the problems facing both civilization and the Earth.

The time may come when the agenda just outlined will look both introspective and limited. We may well have to consider the values of community in galactic terms, when people are living in space stations on the way to colonizing a planet. There is a kind of irony in this possibility in that if the origin of life is to be found, not on Earth, but in the unlimited distances of space, we will be returning to our source. It is also worth keeping in mind the tradition that the germ of the Maya's knowledge of mathematics and astronomy is thought, by some, to be extraterrestrial. However, there is no clear Mayan prophecy of people leaving the Earth to live elsewhere.

Where on Earth Are We?

While the *Popol Vuh* creation myth outlines the characteristics of being human, an individual's sense of self is best fulfilled in the context of community. Community implies place. Whether we live on Earth, on a station suspended in space, or on a colony on Mars, our sense of place and our attachment to it contributes considerably to who we are. The people who lived in crude shelters, desperate to be protected from the elements, dependent on fire, 'the sacred flame', for their survival, are not the same kind of people who occupy hi-tech homes with everything available at the push of a button. But there are more important and more lasting values attached to the notion of location than physical well-being, as is suggested by prophecy 3, which is concerned with the Maya's return to their ceremonial sites. Such places are charged with a special numinous energy, as Hunbatz Men explained:

> There exists four Mayan ceremonial centres of importance the energy of which must be activated so that their energy of light may serve to illuminate the steps humanity must take in this new millennium.[6]

Among the sites recovered in recent times, are Ek Balam, Mayapan, Palenque, Chichén Itzá and Tikal. The recovery, at the ceremonial sites, of 'the sacred energy of the Masters' is, in part, a recovery of the memory of the ancient wisdom. The assembly, already referred to, called by Hunbatz Men at Chichén Itzá in 1995, marked the first phase of the fulfilment of this prophecy. The prophecies were not for the Maya alone, but have universal application, and the call to us is to recognize the spiritual energy focused in the principal sacred sites of all religions. For animistic religions the sense of the sacredness of place is not limited to something that has been built. Mountains, rivers, sacred groves, songlines, ley lines, caves and valleys have all been marked as places of spiritual empowerment. This is not just a characteristic of tribal religion, but a feature found in the beliefs and practices of many New Age faiths. The prophecy is pointing to our need to re-establish a sense of the sacredness of nature and in so doing we may recover part of the wisdom that is lost to us.

— 12 —

WE ONLY KNOW IN PART

In the Mayan scheme of things, as Thorn showed with her maize (corn) metaphor, the quality of the whole is dependent on the quality of every contributing part. Notwithstanding the established divisions with which our world struggles, the community would best be served by people who are comfortable within themselves, at ease in their own skins. Only such rounded individuals would be fit for service in the community and be able to fulfil the roles ascribed to them. Ideally, a person would have attained what Calleman calls 'non-dual cosmic consciousness',[12] a personal 'at-oneness' extended to others and to the whole created universe. Even if the individual is subsumed by the values and needs of society, what kind of person that individual is will count for much. The *Popol Vuh* myth makes it clear that the gods, so as to protect their status and make a necessary distinction between humanity and divinity, withdrew a critical portion of the knowledge originally given to the first humans. In that sense, the individual is flawed and, except for the enlightened few, everyone shares this limitation.

There are many things that distinguish us from other animals: the gifts of thought and speech; reason and reflection; the ability to organize the information we absorb, and to take the decisions that determine individual and collective life. A distinctive, yet dubious mark of being human is that, because of what the gods have done, we are aware the knowledge we have is relative, and thus we live with only a beguiling glimpse of the absolute perception denied us. We are left with a sense of the numinous,[48] a hint that some greater richness of experience is round the corner. This withdrawal or denial of knowledge has implanted in us what David Loy calls, 'a *lack*'.[49] We are, thus, born to the quest, we strive for complete perception, the penny-dropping experience that will fill the void. The Mayan prophecies tell us that throughout our evolution and history, we are slowly spiralling our way upwards towards a complete knowledge of ourselves, reaching for some form of collective maturity. Our inner wholeness, our spiritual development is also a matter of evolution, and the prophecies suggest that this process will climax during the years around 2012.

But this upward journey is not easy. The Maya must have understood how individual kernels of maize would fall away from the cob and lose all relationship to the whole. It goes deeper, since all forms of outer dislocation have their parallels within, in the form of conflicting energies, values, allegiances and priorities. We cannot achieve together what we have not achieved within ourselves.

> Two spirits dwell within my breast
> Each seeks therein its separate existence.
>
> **Goethe**

In its most extreme form this lack of personal inner cohesion can tear us apart.

Living with this sense of lack, of 'something missing', we resort to all manner of devices and sources to fill the void. What the prophecies warn us about is that what we consistently do to compensate for our incomplete knowledge actually blinds us to the perceptions we most need. Materialism and its handmaid, acquisitiveness, are the chief culprits. As prophecy 19 makes clear, we have to transcend a technology that is displacing our natural human facilities. Neanderthal man had a basic toolkit of flint scrapers and hand-axes, and a modest armoury of wooden spears and clubs; 26,000 years later, technology defines the culture in which, by far, the greater number of people live. Raymond

Kurzweil, an inventor and futurist, has made predictions about the extent to which intelligent machines, especially computers and the Internet would mark the territory in which millions would spend the greater part of their lives. In 2001, Kurzweil wrote:

> Within a few decades, machine intelligence will surpass human intelligence, leading to The Singularity – technological change so rapid and profound it represents a rupture in the fabric of human history. The implications include the merger of biological and nonbiological intelligence, immortal software-based humans, and ultra-high levels of intelligence that expand outward in the universe at the speed of light.[50]

Moore's Law, which predicts and describes increases in computer processing power, is also applied to the exponential increase of computer components. Applied to the rate of technological change, the law indicates that speed of change will shortly get close to being infinite, propelling us towards something called 'Singularity'. The Singularity Watch explains the concept as, 'the rise of super intelligent life, created through improvements of human tools by the acceleration of technological progress reaching the point of infinity'.[51] We are at that point already, co-existing with robotics and artificial intelligence and with what Kurzweil calls 'spiritual machines'. Prophecy 19 confronts us with a beguiling question: can machines attain consciousness? The Dalai Lama has an open mind about this:

> I can't totally rule out the possibility that, if all the external conditions and the karmic action were there, a stream of consciousness might actually enter into a computer. There is a possibility that a scientist who has very much involved his whole life with computers, then in the next life he would be reborn a computer. Then this machine which is half-human and half-machine has been reincarnated.[52]

Prophecy 19 is not just concerned with the nature and speed of change, but also with warning us that technology cannot fill the void within us, nor can it ensure the survival of the planet. Furthermore, it is telling us we have not yet come to terms with the relationship between technology and spirituality. All technology carries its own built-in obsolescence, even self-destructive features, and so fast is the speed of change that what is state of the art in the morning, is out of date by the afternoon. Leaving aside spiritual considerations, technology already has an organic relationship with our bodies, for example, pace-makers are implanted to control or correct an erratic heartbeat, machines are used to transfuse or to filter blood, and ventilators (respirators) can sustain life mechanically until the lungs can resume the task. The prospect of the 'lack' being satisfied by technology is interesting, and if applied over long periods of time could conceivably have an effect on our physical evolution as the functions of human organs are given over to machines. There are other more mundane and obvious resources people turn to, if not to fill the void, then as a distraction from its quiet but persistent demands, and to repress the nagging sense that there must be more to life and truth than we have yet grasped: acquisitiveness, money, sex, fame, power are just some of the myriad escapes and distractions available.

The wisdom of which the Maya are custodians is the jealously guarded knowledge that was withdrawn by the gods, and it is the subject of prophecy 14, which speaks of recovered memory. As indicated in an earlier section, we need to look at this more closely. During the critical *katuns* that surround 2012, humanity will begin the process of regaining the insights of which the gods deprived us, and in doing so we will edge towards enlightenment and cosmic consciousness. The Maya, however, while carrying the prophecy of the renewal of consciousness to us, had no access to the discipline of science that has developed in recent times. Science and technology contribute to our understanding of how the prophecies may be fulfilled, but modern psychology resonates closely with the Maya's own perception of who we are, and of the potential we might realize.

The limits of human biology are overcome by mechanical means, terrestrial beings we might be, but we out-fly the birds, we out-swim the fish, and we cruise among the stars. It seems that physically we are in our element wherever we want to be. Is this akin to the omnipresence of the gods? On the other hand, it is easy to feel that computers outstrip human mental ability, and that although the Internet is edging us towards a seeming omniscience, our lost birthright, on the point of recovery, is being usurped. Machines might seem to be intelligent, but such intelligence is artificial. What we are after is the genuine article, the 'real thing', and prophecy 21, in telling us 'we are the prophecy', offers the hope of our regaining just that.

The Chilam Balam of Tizimin accused his contemporaries of forgetting life and 'your own ancient teaching'.[5] The distance of the past, while possibly lending enchantment, also risks the fading of memories. For the Maya, these memories were of the wisdom and knowledge gifted to them, then withdrawn in the moment of creation. Wisdom, like anything else, can be lost through neglect, resulting in spiritual amnesia. The quest for the recovery of wisdom is one shared by most religions. The Maya understood that the loss of wisdom was the root cause of many of their problems. Christianity accounts for this sense of lack as 'original sin', the consequence of which is separation from God. It asks followers to acknowledge their sin, seek forgiveness for it, and accept the propitiatory sacrifice of Christ that frees them from it. The specific theology is broader than its own context in that it relates to the feeling of estrangement so many have from something basic and essential. Buddhism understands that loss of wisdom is due to *avidya*, ignorance, and encourages practitioners to look within for its recovery. The consensus seems to be that the truth of the matter lurks within us, obscured by all the many things we resort to as compensation for our lack of it.

Myths can be carried down the years as vague memories of actual events, or of a time in prehistory when life was simpler. This is not mere nostalgia. The myths encoding actual events are sometimes the expression of tribal memory; all people carry vestiges of this in their subconscious. What the prophecy of recovered memory is therefore telling us, is that we will recover the truths of our original identity, even of our previous existences, as the Dali Lama also assures us:

> It is also possible within this lifetime to enhance the power of the mind, enabling one to re-access memories from previous lives ... Once one has accessed memories of previous lives ... one gradually recalls them in the waking state.[52]

The prophecy of recovered memory speaks of a general, even universal enlightenment. There are however, problems embedded in this prophecy. The final *baktun* is described as a period of 'great forgetting', during which our relationship with nature will, for reasons of ecology and climate change, be seriously impaired. This period of the Fifth Mayan Sun will be marked by extreme materialism, itself obscuring the very truths we want to recover. As if that was not enough, we must recognize that the Western mind will not easily accept Mayan teaching and wisdom, inevitably overlaying it with its own concepts and values. For this reason we are going to have to accept a radical shift in our thinking as, necessarily, we exchange an old belief system for a new one.

'The time', as we say, 'is right', and Carl Jung shared the Mayan sense that we are living at the right moment. 'We are living in what the Greeks called the *kairos* – the right moment – for a 'metamorphosis of the gods', of the fundamental principles and symbols. This peculiarity of our time, which is certainly not of our conscious choosing, is the expression of the unconscious man within us who is changing.'[53]

Who on Earth are we? Until we recover the lost wisdom, God only knows.

PART V

WHAT WILL THE FUTURE BRING?

What will the future bring? From time immemorial this question has occupied men's minds, though not always to the same degree. Historically, it is chiefly in times of physical, political, economic, and spiritual distress that men's eyes turn with anxious hope to the future, and when anticipations, utopias, and apocalyptic visions multiply.

Carl Jung

Congratulations – you are among a select Group of souls who won the lottery to be here, on this planet, at this time! The prize not only ensures you a front row seat but also the unique opportunity to co-create the future of the human race.

Christine Page

This is the way the world ends

Not with a bang but a whimper.

TS Eliot

TS Eliot's poem 'The Hollow Men' took its theme from the Gunpowder Plot and Guy Fawkes' frustrated attempt to blow up the Houses of Parliament. The world, he concludes, will not end so dramatically; the bang with which it started will fade to a whimper, a sob, maybe, for what might have been. There are commentators on the Mayan prophecies who share Eliot's pessimism, but rather than a whimpering end we are warned that what we are heading for is a cataclysmic disaster, even, perhaps the end of life on Earth. This is, in part, supported by the fact that each of the Mayan World Ages (the periods into which the Long Count calendar was divided) ended in catastrophe. The prophecies, carried by the calendars, focus on 21 December 2012, the date which completes the 26,000 years of precession with galactic synchronization, and which concludes the fifth of the Mayan Suns. It seems, then, we are headed for some form of disaster, regional, global or galactic.

The question 'What will the future bring?' must remain open, but it is one that presses and will continue to do so with increasing urgency as we get closer to the 'end date' for the Fifth Sun. The prophecies alert us to certain issues that will either challenge us in life-or-death terms, or demand of us decisions and responsibilities we must assume if life on Earth is to continue in a far better state than 2012 will find it. The question is of such moment that a conference has been called for January 2010 in Cancun, north-eastern Mexico, to which the leading Mayan elders, teachers and specialist scholars have been invited. The conference statement of intention summarizes the question of what we might expect over the next few years.

> 2012 is bringing a good deal of negative and positive speculation as to its significance. Will our sun flare up and knock out our technological/communication base in 2012, causing widespread panic? Will there be objects from space coming to Earth causing death and destruction? Will there be a planetary pole shift? Will we become massively cognisant of other conscious life forms from either space or from other dimensions? Will the first time-machine come

> from particle acceleration experiments causing the future to come roaring into the present? Or, are we going to have a massive wake-up as a species and create something truly wonderful?[54]

The truth is we do not know what the end of this *katun* will bring – the statement's questions cover a wide range of possibilities. Perhaps, after the conference in January 2010, we will have clearer answers about the way the prophecies will be fulfilled, but for the moment, all we can do is to survey the most likely outcome.

— 13 —

'THIS IS THE WAY THE WORLD ENDS'

Prophecy 14 speaks clearly of the destruction of the Earth. The Chilam Balam of Tizimin, leaves us in no doubt about this: 'In the final days of the tying up of the bundle of the thirteen *katuns* on 4 Ahau, then the end of the world shall come.'[5] In some way then, it seems, the Earth itself is at risk. Each of the previous Four Suns ended with some kind of disaster caused, respectively, by water, wind, fire and Earth changes, these latter presumably being earthquakes or volcanic eruption. An alternative reading is given by the Aztec Sun Stone, the glyphs of which have the Four Suns ending with wild animals, wind, fire and water. The possibility of catastrophes is corroborated by geological evidence that shows that every 6,400 years (a quarter of the 25,600-year Long Count calendar) there was a significant disaster caused by floods, earthquakes, volcanoes, fires, or comet impact. Great floods, of course, remind us of the Old Testament story of Noah who was instructed by God to build an ark, and shelter within it his own family and pairs of every living animal, so they might survive God's judgement that the people were wicked (Genesis 6). Another great destruction was that of Atlantis, first described by Plato:

> The island was larger than Libya and Asia put together ... But afterward there occurred violent earthquakes and floods, and in a single day and night of rain all your warlike men in a body sunk into the earth, and the island of Atlantis in like manner disappeared, and was sunk beneath the sea. And that is the reason why the sea in those parts is impassable and impenetrable, because there is such a quantity of shallow mud in the way; and this was caused by the subsidence of the island.[55]

What brought about the destruction of Atlantis (real or mythological, actual history or a Platonic literary device) is thought to have been a combination of earthquake and tsunami, both featuring strongly in our own recent events. Plato lived in the 4th–3rd century BCE, and Atlantis is thought to have disappeared 9,000 years earlier. If Plato was using original or older accounts of the disaster, we have to make allowance for the tradition of writing up local events as if they were universal, as a catastrophe across a large region of what was then the known world. The Genesis flood must certainly have been a local or regional event made to seem universal in order to carry its religious message.

It is more likely that the warning carried by the prophecy of the Earth's demise is not of its total destruction, but one of change – the end of life as we know it. This is not just more plausible, it is also more sensible since, as we have noted, the leitmotif of the prophecies is radical change; and change, while being radical, can also take a fair amount of time. A sudden cataclysm, like the catastrophic eruption in May, 1980, of Mount St Helen's in Washington State, USA, might be a likely event, but the prophecy is concerned with a more general process. Even if 2012 marks the end of the planet, no one is responsibly suggesting that the Earth will somehow disintegrate at sunrise on the winter equinox in December of that year. The Mayan calendars record extremely long periods of time which, because of their inborn character, carry a potential for disaster. The *katun*, while a very important calendric building-block, is merely 20 years in duration, the *baktun*, on the other hand, is 394 years, the current *baktun* having started in 1618 CE, and terminating with the now famous end date of 2012. If there is to be a disaster, it may happen during the years either before or after this date; but the date itself is significant because it marks the end of the cycle of precession and the completion of galactic synchronization.

We need to add one more ingredient to this calendric and numeric recipe of disaster. The Long Count calendar ends with Katun 4 Ahau, whose character is inconsistent and variable, even contradictory. It is the *katun* of making records, of the founding of temple sites such as Chichén Itzá, of crop failure, famine and mortality. It is also the *katun* during which the return of a supreme being is predicted to take place. As the final *katun* of the *baktun,* it is the *katun* of completion, that is, it draws together all the influences of the Katun Ahaus preceding it.

We can summarize what menaces the planet as follows: asteroid impact, changes to the Sun's and Earth's magnetic fields, ecological and climatic disaster, and the return of a supreme being.

Asteroid Impact

One of the more ominous threats to the Earth, featured in disaster movies as well as in responsible science journalism, it that of comet, meteorite or asteroid impact. It is well established that the Earth has already suffered from these. An impact event may have closed the world of the dinosaurs, and there seems reasonable evidence that the Egyptian Old Kingdom and the civilization of Sumeria witnessed these events. Recent research has shown the risk of impacts of this kind is much higher than previously realized.[56] It is not, therefore, a coincidence that there are an increasing number of agencies finding and tracking near-Earth asteroids (NEAs) precisely during the period when the Mayan prophecy warns of the Earth being at risk in this way. These agencies include the Lincoln Near-Earth Asteroid Research laboratory at Massachusetts Institute of Technology, the Near-Earth Asteroid Tracking programme funded by NASA, and the Lowell Observatory Near-Earth Object Search system. Recent impacts include the meteorite that crashed in Troms County, Norway in June 2006 and another that hit the Earth near Carancas, in south-eastern Peru, in September 2007. Other than the risk of impact, there are several reports of asteroids exploding above the air with hugely destructive results. The 'Tunguska event' occurred in June 1908, in the Krasnoyarsk region of Russia. The object, estimated to be tens of metres across, fragmented at a height of 5–10km (3–6miles) with a blast in excess of the Hiroshima bomb. Upwards of a dozen other smaller explosions have been recorded since 1908, the most recent being in October 2008, in the Nubian Desert of Sudan. The possibility of impact, or above-Earth explosion, is being taken very seriously. The International Planetary Defence Conference meets every two years to address the likelihood and consequences of such events. It is comforting to know that not only the tracking of such hazards is on the agenda, but also deflection technologies and contingency plans for aid and survival if such an event should occur.

Changes to the Sun's and Earth's Magnetic Fields

Prophecy 17 also warns of changes to the Earth's magnetic fields. Hunbatz Men has spoken of 'magnetic centres' where sacred teachings were deposited thousands of years ago. These are spread across the world from Chan Chan in Peru to the Isle of Mull in Scotland. He claims, somewhat fancifully, that the names of all these places are of Mayan origin, suggesting that at some time the Maya were present at these sacred magnetic centres.[6] Actual Mayan presence is dubious, but magnetic fields may provide some form of connection between these places.

The Maya lived in fear that the Sun would decline and no longer be able to support life on Earth. They could not have known that it has been active for something in the order of 4.5 billion years and is likely to continue for another

5 billion years. What is being prophesied is not the death of the Sun but an unprecedented change in its behaviour, the effects of which will be felt on Earth. An early sign of this is change to the Earth's magnetic field. The Maya believed that, because of the galactic synchronization that will occur on 21 December 2012, the energy of the Sun would increase and that its light would intensify. Such intensification is known to science as a solar flare, which causes a reversal of the Sun's magnetic field. NASA recorded this happening in 2001, when what is termed 'the solar maximum' of the 11-year cycle was reached.

> The Sun's magnetic poles will remain as they are now, with the north magnetic pole pointing through the Sun's southern hemisphere, until the year 2012 when they will reverse again. This transition happens, as far as we know, at the peak of every 11-year sunspot cycle – like clockwork.[57]

The same thing happens on Earth but only, roughly, every 500,000 years, the last occurring 700,000 years ago. When it does take place, the magnetic field reversal causes an irregularity in the Earth's rotation which can result in natural disasters, such as violent winds, earthquake and volcano eruption. We do not know when the Earth's magnetic poles will reverse again – one calculation is that it will happen in about 1,200 years. It will not be a sudden happening but a gradual process.

The 11-year sunspot cycle was recorded by the Maya throughout the Long Count calendar, and marked to recur in 2012. While there is nothing at all unusual about this, the extent of the Sun's activity in 2012 will be unprecedented. The Sun's own magnetic poles will reverse once more, but NASA is saying that the new solar maximum will be 30–50 per cent greater than any previous geomagnetic storm.

Any such storm will create disturbances in the Earth's magnetosphere, and solar wind shock-waves may strike the Earth's magnetic field only a day or two afterwards. We have to take into account, therefore, that the huge increase in sunspot activity in 2012 will have consequences on Earth, principally in changes to the magnetic field which itself will have knock-on effects including, for example, a reversal of the direction in which water spins out of a sink, or in which a tornado revolves. More importantly, mammals such as dolphins, porpoises and whales use the magnetic poles for navigation, and there is already an increase in the numbers beached because of their sense of direction being confused. Similar problems have been observed for migrating birds and animals, some of which have been discovered at considerable distances from their habitual routes. While the entire Earth may not be at risk, we ought, as with the possibility of comet impact, to have contingency plans in place for serious volcanic eruptions, flooding, wild fires, earthquakes and tsunamis, even for a combination of these. Together, they amount to the 'radical change' theme of the prophecies.

Ecological and Climatic Disaster

The threat to planet Earth is one thing, the threat to the life it sustains is another. We have no control over an asteroid that is heading our way and, apart from the problems caused by the thinning of the ozone layer, we have little control over climate change, which across thousands of years follows its own cycle. Prophecy 16, which speaks of ecology and climate, touches on probably the most immediately relevant and familiar of the prophecy's themes. Rather than being in harmony with nature, we shall be in conflict with it. The consequences of this conflict have been the subject of world media attention for many decades. The fact that we have already become aware of the acuteness of the problem suggests the prophecy is in process of being fulfilled. The agenda of ecological emergency is so well established, there is no need to do more than mention the critical areas: global warming and the melting ice-caps (which may be part of a natural, very long-term cycle), and the extinction of animals and plants at the rate of around a thousand species a year, greater than at any time since dinosaurs trod the earth. This annihilation is mankind's responsibility: our consumption levels have created a crisis for innumerable creatures, plants and natural resources.

A Cree Indian prophecy has it that:

> Only after the last tree has been cut down
> Only after the last river has been poisoned
> Only after the last fish has been caught
> Only then will you find you cannot eat money.

The world's oil supply will last until around 2050, but we are not really prepared for the problems that the loss of it will bring. 'The effects of such a crisis could be exponentially magnified by the side effects of accelerated climate change, resource depletion, military conflicts, and declining food production.'[58] Such warnings as the prophecy brings of Earth, ecology and climate changes, are not as alarming as those hinting at the death of the world itself. The present state of our ecology clearly illustrates, as we have seen, that all these Earth-related prophecies are about a process, rather than a sudden cut-off disaster, but 'process' does not diminish either the extent or urgency of our problems.

Industrialization, the soulmate of technology, has certainly contributed to the ecological and climate change problems which dominate our lives. In terms of the Mayan calendar, we are now living through the final *katun* of the Great Cycle, 1992–2012, a period which will end with the Earth being brought into conjunction with the Milky Way. The Maya's term for this is, 'the Earth's Regeneration Period', so called because it is the time when the planet will be purified and reinvigorated.

We have to believe the Maya are right.

The Return of a Supreme Being

'Would that he might return from the west, uniting us in commiseration over our present unhappy plight! This is the fulfilment of the prophecies of Katun 5 Ahau ... God grant that there may come a Deliverer from our afflictions, who will answer our prayers in Katun 1 Ahau': so wrote the Chilam Balam of Tizimin.[5] The prophecy and expectation of the return of a supreme being is an eschatology shared by all the major religions. It is not, however, a hope that appeals greatly to the modern, secular mind.

The supreme being of whom prophecy 4 speaks is

Quetzalcoatl, known to the Maya as Kukulcan. Much of Mesoamerican mythology is built around Quetzalcoatl, one of the principal gods of the pantheon. His emblem, the feathered or plumed serpent together with the cult it represents is found throughout Mexico and the prophecy of his return is central to Mayan belief. So central was it that, as already pointed out, Montezuma took Cortés, the invading Spaniard, for the returning god.

The *katun* prophecy that spoke clearly of the return of the supreme being is the prophecy of Katun 4 Ahau, through which we are now living and which will terminate the Long Count calendar at the winter equinox of 2012. The Book of Chilam Balam of Chumayel has it that:

> the katun is established at Chichén Itzá.
> The settlement of the Itzá shall take place [there].
> The quetzal shall come, the green bird shall come.
> Ah Kantenal shall come. Blood-vomit shall come.
> Kukulcan shall come with them for the second time. [It is] the word of God.[4]

Blood-vomit was probably yellow fever; it might have been an actual epidemic, or a reference to the 'plague' of the Spanish invasion. It may have been both. The significant point is that Kukulcan is expected to make his reappearance when the world is in most need of him. This is consistent with other 'messianic' hopes. Unsurprisingly, the Spanish missionaries turned the prophecy of Kukulcan's return to their own advantage, explaining that it was a prophecy about the appearance of the Spanish and the Maya's conversion to Christianity. The missionary process has always used indigenous myths and practices where it could as a means of converting the 'heathen'. But the Christianization of the prophecy is easily seen to be superficial, a mere gauze drawn over an ancient native tradition which predates the Spanish influence by many centuries (the prophecy's earliest appearance being dated during the 3rd century ce).

Who, then, was the Mayan god, Kukulcan?

He was first known to the Aztecs as Quetzalcoatl, as a miraculous synthesis of bird and snake, *quetzal* referring to a bird (*Pharomachrus mocinno*) with bright green wing and tail feathers, while *coatl* refers to a serpent, the rattlesnake. The symbolism is multilayered. During the course of his evolution, Kukulcan has been variously thought of as a water spirit or a deity of water, the god of abundance and fertility, the god of the rain-cloud-bringing wind, that is, wind in its life-giving aspect. In late, Post-Classic central Mexico, he was the god of priests, merchants and the patron god of rulers.[60]

The serpent symbolism is significant and has parallels

with the esoteric secret knowledge of Hindu *k'ulthanlilni*, better known as kundalini, the yoga and meditative practice of which uses the seven chakras, the body's energy centres. By this means, practitioners believed they could draw the energy of the Earth and cosmos into the body. That the Maya also knew of the seven power centres of the body raises, again, the question of influence discussed in Part I, but this is more likely to be another example of separate, parallel development. In Hinduism, the kundalini is a serpent-like potential coiled and 'sleeping' at the base of the spine. Once 'awakened' by specialized yoga practice, the energy released rises through the chakras and leads to liberation. In Mayan mythology the path is the same, but the source of the energy is in the Earth, not in the base of the spine. That the liberating energy is sourced in the Earth and passes through the body, creates a vital association between them which offers a graphic image of one of the central themes of the prophecies, that we need to recover our innate relationship with nature.

What, then, does the return of Kukulcan signify? For the Maya, the implications of the prophecy of the god's return go far beyond the myth itself and do not need to be interpreted literally as a 'second coming', or reincarnation. Rather the hope lies in the enlightenment, and the transformation of the consciousness spoken of in prophecies 12 and 13. Through these means, ordinary people will take on the character and attributes of the supreme being through their own spiritual evolution. By the 'initiation of cosmic wisdom ... people can attain the same, high spiritual state, so as to "become" Kukulcan ... We need only develop our faculties of consciousness to full realize that status.'[9] The prophecy is, therefore, one of the recovery of an energy drawn from the Earth, creatively transformed to resolve the many problems we face as we approach 2012. A person 'becoming the god' is a figure of someone transcending an earthbound, materialistic way of life. The mythology that wraps the prophecy brings us back to the cycles of Venus (*see* prophecy 9) as it is these that signal the return of Kukulcan after 'five full cycles of the dawn star', (i.e. Venus as the morning star). As we have noted, the galactic synchronization set for 21 December 2012 will be preceded by a transit of Venus across the face of the Sun on 6 June of that year.

Although the scribes recording the prophecies in the various Books of the Chilam Balam used different names for 'god', they were concerned to represent Kukulcan, the one god, standing behind them. Like all other religions, Mayan religion evolved, and in the texts we are able to trace the beginnings of the transition from polytheism, to the monotheism of the one supreme god, Hunab K'u. Following the Post-Classic demise of the Maya, their civilization and culture flourished once more, a process aided by this trend to monotheism, the one god becoming symbolic of one people. However, the process was completed, not by the natural evolution of their religion, but by having monotheism forced upon them in the form of the Catholicism of the Spanish invaders. The return of a supreme being is a common theme in the eschatology of the major world religions and carries the hope, for example, of a Jewish Messiah, a Christian Saviour, an Islamic Mahdi, a Hindu Kalki, or the Maitreya Buddha. Such a return is usually anticipated for the time when the world and humanity will be at risk; a terminal moment of judgement and salvation.

To do justice to this prophecy, there is one further theme to be added. The concept of the return of a supreme being carries something of triumphalism with it, the idea that 'good' will overcome 'evil', 'love' will overcome 'hate', 'God' will defeat 'the Devil'. The problem with triumphalism is that it reinforces the view that the whole of life is a battle between these opposing forces. It is an attitude based on rigorous dualism. However, there are movements in Judaism, Christianity and Sufi Islam that, like the Mayan elder Hunbatz Men, interpret the 'messianic expectation' in terms not of political or religious triumphalism, but as a process of evolving consciousness. Buddhism has always taken this latter view. Furthermore, the return of a supreme being does not accord with a circular view of time but with the 'climax' of a linear view of time. The evolution of consciousness will overcome the restraints of dualism, and the sense of our being up against the other will change to a sense of our being at one with the other. Separation, Buddhism teaches, is an illusion. It is in this way that prophecies about enlightenment and cosmic consciousness will be fulfilled. If every human being realized their non-duality, the world in which we live would transform to the degree the prophecies tell us it must if we are to survive. There is, of course, a considerable problem to overcome, as religious fundamentalism is sustained by preserving the status quo; by definition fundamentalists abhor the idea that religious doctrine can evolve – such change is at loggerheads with orthodoxy. The need to be right takes precedence over the need for truth.

The move from the expectation of a literal return of a supreme being to the evolution of consciousness is radical indeed. It anticipates the non-dual recognition of the truths inherent in both religious and secular ideals, and to what Jay Michaelson calls 'a biodiversity of spirit that, as in ecology, nourishes the whole by supporting difference'.[61]

— 14 —

REDEEMING THE TIME

In Part II, mention was made of the need to redeem time, specifically for those *katuns* characterized by negative energies and tendencies. *The katun*, as we have seen, is the basic 20-year calendric building block, each of which has its own character. The name of the *katun* was taken from the day name of the *tzolk'in* calendar on which it ended, and because of the cycling a *katun* always ends on Ahau, but with a different number until the cycle is complete. The following summary, compiled by Bruce Scofield from the Books of Chilam Balam of Chumayel, Mani and the Codex Perez, illustrates how each *katun* has a distinctive personality, with only Katun 12 Ahau showing a positive tendency:

> Katun 11-Ahau: Apparently food is scarce during this katun and invading foreigners arrive and disperse the population. There is an end to traditional rule, there are no successors. Since this is the first katun it always opens up a new era. It was

during the span of this katun that the Spanish began their takeover of Yucatan and imposed Christianity on the natives.

Katun 9-Ahau: This is a period of bad government where the ruler abuses his people and commits misdeeds. Rulers are so bad that they wind up losing some of their power to the priests. Carnal sin and adultery are practiced openly, by rulers and others, and it is also a time of wars. It is the katun of the 'forcible withdrawal of the hand', a phrase the meaning of which is unclear.

Katun 7-Ahau: This is apparently a time of social excess including drinking and adultery, a low point in the history of the society. Governments stoop to their lowest. The 'bud of the flower', an allusion to eroticism, is said to sprout during this katun.

Katun 5-Ahau: During this katun of misfortune, rulers and their subjects separate – the people lose faith in their leaders. Leaders may be harshly treated, even hung. There is also an abundance of snakes, a great famine, and few births during this period.

Katun 3-Ahau: This katun brings changes and calamities such as drought and wars. The people will become homeless and society will disintegrate.

Katun 1-Ahau: This katun brings even worse troubles, weak rulers and destruction. Governments fall apart due to rivalries. There may also be a great war which will end and brotherhood will return.

Katun 12-Ahau: During this period government and rulers are wise. Poor men become rich and there is abundance in the land. There is friendship and peace in the land. There will be six good years followed by six bad before well-being returns.

Katun 10-Ahau: Although this is a holy katun, there is trouble in the land once again. This katun brings drought and famine and is a time of foreign occupation, calendar change, and sadness.

Katun 8-Ahau: This may be the worst of the katuns as both Chichén Itzá and Mayapan, the two great ruling cities of Yucatan, were destroyed during its period. The texts speak of demolition and destruction among the governors, an end to greed, but much fighting. It is the katun of 'settling down in a new place.'

Katun 6-Ahau: This is a time of bad government and deceptive government. There is also starvation and famine.

Katun 4-Ahau: There will be scarcities of corn and squash during this katun and this will lead to great mortality. This was the katun during which the settlement of Chichén Itzá occurred, when the man-god Kukulcan (Quetzalcoatl) arrived. It is the katun of remembering and recording knowledge, of pestilence, 'blood vomit shall come', and the *katun* that introduces a new world or world age.

Katun 2-Ahau: For half of the katun there will be food, for half some misfortunes. This katun brings the end of the 'word of God.' It is a time of uniting for a cause.

Katun 13-Ahau: This is a time of total collapse where everything is lost. It is the time of the judgement of God. There will be epidemics and plagues and then famine. Governments will be lost to foreigners and wise men, and prophets will be lost.[62]

There is nothing mystical or mythological about how the *katuns* earned their reputation. The given character is entirely due to what actually happened during the continuing recurrences of the 20-year period, over long periods of time, cycled 13 times, thus over 260 years. Bruce Scofield has also provided the dates (on the Gregorian calendar) during which, over the past 1,000 years, the *katuns* have been cycled, the 20-year period being read vertically.

13 Ahau	1007	1263	1520	1776	2032
11 Ahau	1027	1283	1539	1796	2052
9 Ahau	1046	1303	1559	1815	
7 Ahau	1066	1322	1579	1835	
5 Ahau	1086	1342	1598	1855	
3 Ahau	1106	1362	1618	1874	
1 Ahau	1125	1382	1638	1894	
12 Ahau	1145	1401	1658	1914	
10 Ahau	1165	1421	1677	1934	
8 Ahau	1185	1441	1697	1953	
6 Ahau	1204	1460	1717	1973	
4 Ahau	1224	1480	1736	1993	
2 Ahau	1244	1500	1756	2012	

The prophecy based, for example, on Katun 13 Ahau is determined by its character, as described above. We can see that one of the cycles of this *katun* began in 1520, for which Chilam Balam of Tizimin prophesied, 'A strong man seizes the land ... the battle flag is raised ... the foreigners descended from the sea ... in 8 Ahau,'[3] that is, in the eighth year of the *katun*. Chilam Balam of Chumayel adds, 'This was the katun when the foreigners arrived. They came from the East ... Then Christianity also began ...'[4] The accuracy of this prophecy of the Spanish invasion is as remarkable as is its consistency with the character of the *katun*. The *katun* that began in 1776 was blighted by the War of American Independence, the war between England and France, the second Mysore war, the Peruvian rebellion against Spanish rule, the Japanese famine which reduced the population by a million, the Austrian war against Turkey, and the period ended with the French Revolution.

The *katun* through which we are now living, Katun 4 Ahau, which terminates in 2012, is the *katun* of completion. Its prophecy speaks, among other things, of the return of a supreme being.

It seems the reputation of a *katun* accumulates, it rolls on with time. The question then is, can the character of a *katun* be changed, can its time be redeemed, and if so, how?

Redeeming the time has a direct bearing on what the future holds, because what is involved is not buying or winning back the time, but changing the present *katun* so as to ensure a more positive future. Whether or not we can change the character of a *katun* depends on the extent to which its character is permanently set. If its character is inviolable, then there is nothing we can do about it and we are left with trying to limit its negative influences and encouraging those that are more positive. If the personality of a *katun* can be changed by, for example, the way we live, by our priorities, commitments and perseverance, then the responsibility for what the future will bring is entirely in our hands. In an important way, what we are concerned with is determinism and freedom.

The Mayan message, of course, casts all of this in a broader astrological context, since the *katuns* and *baktuns* of the calendars represent the greater cycles of the stars and planets. Both the actual and symbolic influence of these are carried to our own character according to our date, place and time of birth. It is likely that human life, in its most positive form, is a process of first recognizing, and then harmonizing with these determining planetary influences. There are, however, other determining influences. While we live and behave as human animals, rather than natterjack toads or Venus fly-traps, we each have a DNA that distinguishes us from all other humans. It is within the determining influence of our DNA that we try to live in harmony with the planets and with all other sentient beings. It can be argued that in as much as we can change, or adapt ourselves to achieve this harmony, so can we influence the times in which we live, and in that process change the character of the *katun*. It is a matter of deciding whether these influences are a form of predestination, or are a potential for the realization of which we have some form of control. What we decide will depend on the extent to which we bring our knowledge and wisdom to bear on this balance-harmony-potential-freedom equation. The more we are aware of the forces determining our characters and lives, the more intelligent we can be in our response to and use of them. It is the difference between living in what Buddhism calls *avidya*, 'ignorance' or 'delusion', responding blindly to whatever life throws up, and being *bodhi*, 'awakened', responding with minds constantly open and aware. It is here that the Mayan message calls us back again, to the recovery of lost knowledge, to the possibility of enlightenment and a renewed form of consciousness.

We can redeem the time only to the extent to which we can redeem ourselves.

— 15 —

PROPHECY AND EVOLUTION

The end of the precessional cycle of 26,000 years that returns the galaxy to alignment is not a Mayan prediction or prophecy, but an astronomical event calculated and plotted in the Mayan calendars. The prophecy is to be found in how they interpreted the event of galactic synchronization. As John Major Jenkins pointed out, 'The Maya understood that whereas the 260-day sacred cycle is our period of individual gestation, the 26,000 year cycle is our collective gestation – our collective unfolding as a species.'[13] It is, in a sense, a prophecy of evolution, though the 'unfolding' is not simply a matter of biological evolution, but concerns the further development of our mental, emotional and intuitive faculties. In this 'unfolding', prophecy has a part to play, not simply with regard to biological evolution, but with the future development of our emotional, intuitive, spiritual and mental faculties.

The Evolution of the Mind

The evolution of the mind is a controversial subject associated with evolutionary psychology (EP), the question being not that the mind evolves, but how? Charles Darwin theorized that the mind developed through a process of gradual adaptation to the demands of a constantly changing environment over long periods of time. For our most distant ancestors, physical survival was their most pressing need, and hunting for food, gathering fuel for fires, securing shelter, and breeding were their central occupations. These basic life requirements were what focused and formed the nature of their minds and Darwin argued that the mind, like the body, evolves through natural selection of those functions that assure survival. We cannot, from this assertion, make comparisons between these earlier minds and our own, as we have no evidence whatsoever of the psychological disposition or traits of our ancestors, or of what functions of the mind were subjected to the adaptive process.

Significantly for the Mayan prophecies about enlightenment and consciousness, our minds exist in an environment radically different from that of early humans, an environment that is not only constantly changing, but doing so at an unprecedented rate. Many human groups are still occupied with the demands of physical survival due, for example, to a combination of famine, natural disaster and war. Generally, in the Western world, unless we are taken with a life-threatening illness, physical survival is not our main concern. The majority are preoccupied with surviving economically, and with maintaining a certain standard of living. It would make an interesting research project to enquire into how this preoccupation with economic survival, with securing material well-being, affects the development of the mind.

The modern mind is increasingly conditioned by scientific rationalism. Ironically, although that same mind has produced the most extraordinary culture of technology, it is near to the point of being in service to what it has created. Over a long period of time, the mind has had to adapt to the huge differences between, for example, the Neanderthal environment and the hi-tech environment, and through this process of adaptation the mind itself has evolved. What this evolution of the mind implies is that we have radically changed our broader, cultural environment and, in the process, have changed ourselves. A consequence of this is that while Neanderthal man was wholly and necessarily part of the greater environment in which he lived (entirely integrated with nature) we hold ourselves apart from it by means of a kind of conscious and contrived objectivity.

Originally, human beings cooperated with nature, now (we believe) we control it. It is this change, this transition, that is the concern of the prophecies dealing with evolution and genetics, with consciousness, and with the recovery of memory.

Computers may have the potential to develop intelligence greater than our own, performing, across a huge range of disciplines, functions that we would once have undertaken ourselves, as well as others that are quite beyond our mental capacities. The mind, thus relieved, is 'free' to take on other roles. If the mind does evolve through natural selection, we need to consider what functions of mind will ensure our survival as human beings in contexts other than a technological environment. As discussed in Part IV, developing the capacity to think was a critical moment in human evolution, and one that saw the beginnings of the dominance of intellect at the expense of instinct. The path taken by our enquiring minds led, eventually, to the technocracy in which we now live. In following that path we have failed to develop other potentials of the mind, for example, telekinesis and telepathy. It is too early to say if such 'paranormal' functions can be fully developed alongside science and technology. Certainly when we see such things in practice, we are mostly inclined to dismiss them as chicanery. But prophecy 13, which speaks of cosmic consciousness, implies new applications of mental energy and new ways of thinking. All development is a form of evolution, and this prophecy rests on the idea that the evolution of the mind runs parallel to physical evolution.

The running theme of the Mayan prophecies is that to survive in any lasting and worthwhile way, our minds must turn to our spiritual potential. This has little to do with religions in their established forms; it has to do with relationship, personal, collective and cosmic, not as we have seen, with the idea of each of us being an integral part of whole, but with the experience of it. In realizing this, we can see that prophecy itself is a function of evolution.

The Evolution of Consciousness

Given that one of the leading themes of the Mayan prophecies is the transformation of consciousness how, then, are we to understand consciousness itself, and what does its transformation mean?

Consciousness is usually thought to be the state we are all in when our senses are functioning normally. That is, consciousness is seen to be an addition of physical, mental and emotional responses to what we see, hear, touch, taste and smell. Our senses make us aware of things. Consciousness is known to work beyond the range of our physical senses; it is one of the features that sets us apart from other animals. Animals, in terms of being physically aware, are conscious across a whole range of stimuli, but there are significant levels of experience to which they do not have access because they are not conscious of them. We are, again, on the edge of controversy as there are many who would be reluctant to accept that animals lack the 'higher' consciousness we claim for ourselves. Furthermore, we bring to our consciousness of people, nature, things and ideas, a moral and aesthetic response as well as a whole system of values and judgements set by both our culture in general, and the subculture of each individual. For animals, a sunset will trigger responses associated with night, hunting, territory, safety, rest and so on. These are all genetically embedded and conditioned, but no animal would be aware of the beauty of a sunset that inspires poetry, music, love, reflection and a sense of well-being. Most people would find it impossible to restrict a conscious response to a sunset merely to what strikes our eyes, our reaction goes beyond the physical input, and includes how the event is received and processed by our disposition, and the knowledge and experience we already have. The different ways we react, subtle and refined as they may now be, imply that whatever consciousness is, it has been subjected to a long evolutionary process.

The moral and aesthetic aspect of consciousness carries the human mind beyond the merely mundane to another dimension of reality. The Maya, because of the differences of culture and environment, might not have experienced the same aesthetic response to the sunset, especially as this would be preceded, or quickly followed, by the rising of Venus, the evening star, with all the fearsome associations it carried to them. Significantly, though, prophecy 13 speaks of a different level or order of consciousness, namely, cosmic consciousness. For the Maya, this was nothing rarefied or exceptional; it was the founding principle of their culture. It is greatly encouraging that the prophecy dares to suggest that we, in our own time, could be touched by this form of consciousness. What it amounts to is a meeting of cosmic and meditative modes of consciousness, that is, of the macro and micro aspects of consciousness. In the view of Arthur Koestler, individual consciousness is a fragment of cosmic consciousness, the trick is for the individual to know this and to live accordingly. Our individual consciousness, the level at which we live most of our lives, is full of fixed constructs which inhibit any chance we might have of seeing underlying patterns of alternative perception.

The Evolution of Spirituality

Spirituality is not a religion. It is a form of energy found at the heart of all true religious practice, the sole aim and purpose of which is the cultivation of its strength and quality. It is easier to understand spirituality's concerns when set against other values such as materialism, dogmatism and authoritarianism. In Western culture, spirituality and the 'things of the spirit' imply a deeply entrenched dualism, mentioned briefly earlier, which is represented by the usual labels: God and the Devil, good and evil, heaven and earth, saint and sinner, light and darkness, flesh and spirit. These pairings not only catalogue dualism, they set up the whole of life, even secular life, as a conflict between the archetypes waged on the battlefield of everyone's mind and soul. These concepts, and all the religious systems based upon them, have evolved together with the idea of God, which has undergone a radical change since the earliest days of animism and polytheism. The inner energy of spirituality has been part of that evolution, and while it does not figure as the theme of one of the prophecies, it underlies all of them.

The Maya were not deeply spiritual people. As we have seen, their culture was marked by violence and brutality. Their pre-Columbian polytheistic nature religion was in the process of evolving from a holistic pantheism to a dynamic cosmology driven by the sense of a single energy running through and supporting the entire universe. In the West we call this energy 'God'; the Maya called it Hunab K'u, the giver of movement and measure. The name means 'solitary god' or 'sole god', suggesting the beginning of a trend to monotheism. What distinguishes the Mayan nature-related pantheism from other forms is that its context was a sophisticated concept of time and space, centuries ahead of its time, and the calendars that made the concept concrete should be read as sacred literature. We shall never know how the indigenous Mayan religion might have evolved if Spanish Catholicism had not imposed itself on their culture. However, in those places where the old practices and beliefs are still current, such as Guatemala, a real seam of spirituality is in evidence. 'All spirituality takes time', says Roberto Poz, a Mayan priest.

> To know the calendar, and to deepen one's understanding of the calendar, takes time. That is, time to get the threads of one's life straightened and in order. Time to understand the relationships in life. Time to know one's capacities and to deepen one's life. Time to feel the forces of spirituality. After a while, you begin to feel the calendars in your body.[44]

Evolution, as a mechanism for survival, marks changes in the development of a species brought about by necessary adaptation to shifts in habitat, climate and the wider environment. This being so, the question we must ask is: to what extent is spirituality indispensable to our survival? Is our need of spiritual energy so vital that the future of the human race is dependent on its cultivation? In short, has a spiritual DNA evolved in our genetic make-up that instructs us to develop a spiritual faculty? The Kabbalah teaches that we all have *reshimo*, a kind of spiritual gene.

> In every point in the heart there is a chain of Reshimot, a stream of data, spiritual situations, that the soul must go through in order to rise from the lowest situation to the highest, i.e. the degree of the Creator.[63]

It is as if the new *reshimot* arise at every moment, setting up a chain reaction that constantly changes our perception and experience, directing our spiritual evolution to the goal of connecting with the force, or energy, of creation. The Kabbalah calls this 'adhesion to the creator'. Belief in reincarnation also implies something like a spiritual DNA, especially in the Tibetan Buddhist tradition founded on the belief that the spirituality of a Dali Lama is carried over into his next reincarnation. Genesis 5:1 offers a similar idea: 'This is the record of Adam's line. When God created man, He made him in the likeness of God.' Spiritual DNA is the imprint on human beings of the divine.

Everyone has a spiritual potential. Realizing a mature spirituality is one of the built-in purposes of life, indispensable if we are to survive purposefully.

PART VI

2012 AND BEYOND

I must mention a challenge that is, I believe, the most dreadfully threatening to psychologists. It is the very strong possibility that there is more than one 'reality' ... in which time and space have vanished, a world in which we cannot live, but whose laws we can learn and perceive, a reality that is based not on our senses but on our inner perceptions.

Carl Rogers

The cosmic man must be restored, the whole man who is made in the image and likeness of the arch-force, which you may call God. This man thinks with his heart and not with party dogma. As I have explained before, there is an order in the universe – a cosmic order – and humans have the possibility of understanding these laws.

Albert Einstein

There is a revolution underway in how we understand ancient Maya metaphysics, astronomy, and other traditions related to 2012. 2012 is about transformation and renewal on a global scale.

John Major Jenkins

A person with an experience is never at the mercy of a person with an argument, but a problem arises when that person wants to share the experience in such a way as to demonstrate its validity. We are faced with the perennial question, what is truth, and how are we to demonstrate it objectively? It is not the purpose of this book to explore the possible answers to these questions, or to discuss the principles of verification and, yet, living as we do in a world sceptical of such things, we all want to know if there is 'truth' in the Mayan prophecies. For Mayan history, mythology, religion, astronomy and social organization, we can confidently rely on the thoroughly researched works of anthropologists like Michael Coe, Linda Schele, and Barbara

Tedlock; so that we can understand what the surviving codices actually say, Ralph Roys and M W Makemson have comprehensively researched and translated their hieroglyphs. However, it is the work of scholars such as John Major Jenkins and José Argüelles that takes us into the territory between science and abstraction, between rationalism and intuitive insight. They offer the view from a place where, perhaps, most of us will stand, having surveyed the scene as fully as possible, reflecting on the information, and making up our own minds. The outcome will never be 'all or nothing'. As with many other ideas that confront us, there will be aspects we simply can't live with, while there will be others that resonate strongly with the perceptions we already have, or which, as it were, open our eyes. Still others will agree with the 18th-century German scientist and satirist, Georg C Lichtenberg:

> There exists a species of transcendental ventriloquism by means of which men can be made to believe that something said on earth comes from Heaven.[64]

— 16 —

THE ENDURING MESSAGE

Of one thing we can be quite certain: the problems the Mayan prophecies point to are real. When the prophecies are put together, they offer a fairly accurate description of the current state of human affairs, the condition of the planet and the escalating risks to which all forms of life are exposed. That being so, we have little to lose in considering our response. Most people have, individually and collectively, an almost adolescent resistance to being told (or even advised) what to do, except when that advice has been asked for. And it is easy to react with disbelief to what scientists, politicians and social commentators are telling us. We are caught, for example, between the worst-case scenario of global warming, melting ice-caps, the extinction of innumerable species of animals, war and the rumour of war; and the rationalized, 'things aren't as bad as they say they are' syndrome, which is accounted for by arguments telling us that climate change is part of a recurring, long-term natural cycle, and that the disappearance of animals is also a natural process that, as any palaeontologist might demonstrate, has precedents.

What, then, are the enduring themes of the Mayan prophecies?

Hidden Likenesses

> All science is the search for unity in hidden likenesses ... The scientist looks for order in the appearances of nature by exploring such likenesses, for order does not display itself [automatically]; if it can be said to be there at all it is not there for the mere looking ... Order must be discovered and in a deep sense it must be created. We remake nature by the act of discovery in the poem or in the theorem.[65]

For many, the core of the prophecies that will stand the test of time are what Bronowski calls 'hidden likenesses'. Much of the prophecies are about just this, the description of 'likenesses', and the prophecies themselves disclose these likenesses by demonstrating the extent to which their message resonates with a science and a technology to which the prophets had no access. Three illustrations of hidden likeness will be sufficient to make the point clear.

The first example relates to the mythology and prophecy

about the Milky Way (prophecy 13) with its reference to the 'dark rift', part of which was seen by the Maya as the mouth of a monster, a cave, the crater of a volcano, or the entrance to the underworld. Only relatively recently has it been discovered that at the centre of the Milky Way there is a supermassive black hole, Sagittarius A*. We now know that black holes began as stars, gigantic nuclear generators that, despite their incalculable power and longevity, die. They implode, leaving the void we call a 'black hole'. Every galaxy has one huge black hole and uncountable small ones. The implications of this presence in our galaxy remain the subject of research; we know only that anything drawn into a black hole, even light, can never get out.

The Maya did not understand at all what we barely understand ourselves; by naked-eye observation they sensed this galactic presence to be of huge significance, and they developed a central part of their mythology around it as a means of giving it a description and an identity to which they could relate. For the Maya, the 'mouth' of the 'dark rift' was a menace, an ominous location in the sky. Everything we so far know about the black hole confirms this perception, although we resort to science, rather than to mythology, to understand it; the prophecy has disclosed its hidden likeness. The marked difference between the Mayan and modern perception of the Milky Way's 'cave' or 'black hole', shows the extent to which the act of observing changes both what is observed and the observer.

The second example is evolution, the subject discussed in chapter 15, 'Prophecy and Evolution'. We know that the physical evolution of human beings is unlikely to have reached its zenith. In whatever way this might continue, Mayan prophetic insight has indicated that our minds will continue to evolve so as to realize the potential of virtually dormant faculties, as well as developing a new and heightened consciousness. These are the subjects of prophecies 12, 13 and 14. If Bronowski is right, and science is looking for a unity in the hidden likenesses, then in these prophecies what is observable is unity in the form of a pattern in the message the prophecies make known. Carl Rogers, the American psychologist, put it this way:

> When a pattern is sensed, it must be perceived in its *own* terms; whether those terms are internal, ineffable, subjective, and invisible; or whether they are external, tangible, and visible ... I regard this sensing of a pattern of relationships as perhaps the heart of all true science.[66]

We might add, it is also the heart of all true prophecy.

Such a 'pattern of relationship', can be clearly traced from the Chilam who channelled the prophecies to the contemporary Mayan elders and day-keepers who interpret them. The pattern travels not only across this long period of time, but within the themes of the prophecies themselves, especially those with which we are presently concerned: they speak of enlightenment, consciousness, and, the third example, recovered memory. The ongoing development of the mind is consistent with the basic principle of evolution: to ensure survival. The question is, will our minds will adapt rapidly enough to make the necessary response to what threatens the planet?

An interesting hidden likeness can be found in the recovery of past-life memories. Such an idea will push the belief of many people to its limits, and yet research into child subjects has thrown up some arresting results.[67] It seems that when we are young, our past-life memories are played out in speech, games, drawings, accepted by the adult world as 'natural' child fantasy.

> At the University of Virginia, we've studied over 2,500 cases of children who seem to talk about previous lives when they're little. They start at 2 or 3, and by the time they're 6 or 7, they forget all about it and go on to live the rest of their lives.[68]

Prophecy 14, which speaks of recovered memory, seems to be a clear disclosure of this otherwise hidden likeness. Apparently, it is only because our minds become overlaid with layer after layer of constantly accruing data that, as adults, we do not remember previous lives. The prophecy suggests that such memories are recoverable, together with the wisdom that has eluded us, as discussed in chapter 12 'We only Know in Part'.

Intuitive Sensing

> The fact that modern physics, the manifestation of an extreme specialisation of the rational mind, is now making contact with mysticism, the essence of religion and manifestation of an extreme specialisation of the intuitive mind, shows very beautifully the unity and complementary nature of the rational and intuitive modes of consciousness; of the yang and the yin.
>
> Fritjof Capra[69]

To fully appreciate the message of the Mayan prophecies, we need to be sensitive to different ways of knowing. Epistemology attempts to answer the questions of what knowledge is, how we acquire it, what we really know, and how we know what we know. Such matters are beyond the scope of this book and all we need to be aware of here is that there are different ways of knowing, that is there are different 'experiences' of learning. For example, we can learn from observation, reading, listening, from direct teaching or coaching, from other people's or our own experiences, from inner reflection, and from developing self-knowledge, which we acquire through all of these. Chapter 11, 'Thinking the Right Thing', touched on the difference between knowledge and belief. Belief can be 'hard' knowledge, as when we say, 'I believe the Earth is round', knowing quite well that it is. It can be 'soft' knowledge, as when we say, 'I know about prophecy, but I don't *believe* in it'. In a word, belief is subjective, dependent on a person's perceptions; truth is objective, completely independent of any individual insight or qualification. Both, however, are different kinds of knowledge.

The prophecies demonstrate these different forms of knowing. Their statements about the state of the planet, materialism and technology are objectively verifiable descriptions. If we want to do real justice to the message and meaning of those prophecies that speak to us of consciousness, enlightenment and recovered memory, we are going to have to listen to our intuition, that is, to that sense which gives us a perception of the truth, independently of the process of reasoning. We might use the alternative terms 'sudden insight' or 'immediate apprehension'. There are people who appear to have a heightened sense of intuition, others who never seem to operate at this level. A core teaching of Eastern philosophy, specifically certain traditions of Buddhism, is that the gateway to truth is something other than the mind: intuition.

> If you use your mind to try and understand reality,
> you will understand neither your mind nor reality.
> If you try and understand reality without using
> your mind,
> you will understand both your mind and reality.[70]

Certainly, to appreciate the message of the prophecies we are going to have to open our minds and move out of our conditioned patterns of thought. The great documentary filmmaker, Francis Flaherty (quoted by Carl Rogers[66]) offers this description of how intuition can cut through our habitual constructs and confront us with a new truth.

> What you have to do is let go, let go every thought

> of your own, wipe your mind clean, fresh, innocent, newborn, sensitive as unexposed film to take up the impressions around you, and let what will come in. This is the pregnant void, the fertile state of no-mind. This non-preconception, the beginning of discovery.

The prophecies themselves speak of the coming of new forms of knowledge and consciousness; new ways of thinking will follow.

The Ever-present Potential

> For, as the perceptible things which appear in the outside world make us remember what we knew before, so do sensory experiences, when consciously realized, call forth intellectual notions that were already present inwardly; so that that which formerly was hidden in the soul, as under the veil of potentiality, now shines therein in actuality.[71]

Johannes Kepler, the 16th–17th-century German mathematician, astronomer and astrologer, could have had the Mayan prophecies and their message in mind when he was writing of the ever-present potential 'formerly hidden in the soul'. It is hidden no longer. In another sense, that same potential is carried by our genes, and everything in the prophecies that resonates with evolution should be the source of strength and hope for humanity. Mention has been made of an evolving spirituality underlying the Mayan prophecies. Apart from the Chilam, the priests who channelled those prophecies, there is little evidence to suggest theirs was a spiritually enlightened civilization. We cannot know if they had any sense of their own 'lack', or if they hungered after something better than the fear-driven practices that, to us, seem so cruel. There are modern Mayan communities that show a deep-founded sense of spirituality, as if all that is best of the 'old ways' has been carried down the years to them, to the point where, as Jean Molesky-Poz puts it, 'faith now informs life'.[44] The prophecies are in part a summary of that spiritual intent, and in recording them for posterity it is hard to resist the idea that the Chilam, sensible to their own potential, were sharing their vision and wistful testimony of what might have been; and what, for us, must be if we are to survive in any worthwhile and meaningful way.

Mention should be made of modern initiatives concerned with new kinds of potential. 'Transhuman' (i.e. 'transitory human') refers to an evolutionary transition from human to post-human. The term was coined by Fereidoun M Esfandiary (1930–2000) himself a prophet whose prediction of social trends, such as globalization, in vitro fertilization, the correction of genetic weaknesses, teleshopping and the Internet, have proved to be remarkably accurate. Echoing, perhaps, Stephen Hawking's 'Why do we remember the past and not the future?', Esfandiary wrote, 'I have a deep nostalgia for the future'. He believed that various present-day phenomena indicated the evolutionary appearance of transhumans: reconstructive surgery; intense use of telecommunications; a rejection of the usual social and family relationships and values; universalist, cosmopolitan attitudes; and mass travel. The transhuman will be someone prescient of radical future potentials, and who plans ahead for them, who is obsessive about self-enhancement. As these characteristics multiply in our society, a transhuman culture will be created.

'Transhumanism' refers to philosophies of life that define and describe the acceleration of the evolution of intelligent life beyond human limits by means of science and technology. The ruling principle is the ethical use of technology to transcend these limits. The movement, which has an international dimension, views all forms of disability, disease, ageing, mental limitation, even involuntary death, as 'unnecessary' and 'undesirable'. Whether or not such things are unnecessary is debatable, but most would agree they are undesirable.

Both of these potential-realizing initiatives have echoes in the Mayan prophecies, and they have reverberated throughout this book. Both of them, in a sense, are not new at all, but are represented in the human aspiration typical of classical mythology, the quest for immortality; the elixir of life taken up by the alchemists; the values and hopes of Renaissance humanism and the Enlightenment.

We can ask for no better summary than Pico della Mirandola's affirmation, *Oration on the Dignity of Man*, given to the philosopher's debate he called in 1486.

> Neither a fixed abode nor a form that is thine alone nor any function peculiar to thyself have we given thee, Adam, to the end that according to thy longing and according to thy judgment thou mayest have and possess what abode, what form, and what functions thou thyself shalt desire. The nature of all other beings is limited and constrained within the bounds of laws prescribed by Us. Thou, constrained by no limits, in accordance with thine own free will, in whose hand We have placed thee, shalt ordain for thyself the limits of thy nature. We have set thee at the world's centre that thou mayest from thence more easily observe whatever is in the world. We have made thee neither of heaven nor of earth, neither mortal nor immortal, so that with freedom

> of choice and with honour, as though the maker and moulder of thyself, thou mayest fashion thyself in whatever shape thou shalt prefer. Thou shalt have the power to degenerate into the lower forms of life, which are brutish. Thou shalt have the power, out of thy soul's judgment, to be reborn into the higher forms, which are divine.

Regardless of whether we believe or are sceptical, something of the Mayan prophecies holds the attention of millions of people, a number likely to increase the nearer we get to 2012. The Mayan prophecies speak of our potential for personal divinity; they speak of the potential of the transformation of our consciousness; they speak of the evolutionary potential of human senses and faculties as yet barely developed and they speak of a recovered sense of oneness with nature in its universal totality. The abiding message calls us to make a concerted effort to realize these potentials. If we do not, all we will be left with is reduced life, a decaying planet, and the memory of hope.

REFERENCES AND FURTHER READING

1 Aurelius, Marcus, *Meditations*, Wordsworth Classics, 1997

2 Eliade, Mircea, *Shamanism*, Arkana Penguin, London, 1989

3 Roys, Ralph, *The Prophecies for the Maya Tuns or Years in The Books of Chilam Balam of Tizimin and Mani*, Carnegie Institute of Washington, Publication 585, 1949

4 Roys, Ralph L (trans), *The Book of Chilam Balam of Chumayel*, University of Oklahoma Press, 1976

5 Makemson, M W (trans), *The Book of the Jaguar Priest: A Translation of the Book of Chilam Balam of Tizimin*, Henry Schuman, New York, 1951

6 Hunbatz Men, *Mayan Prophecies for the New Millennium*, www.13moon.com

7 Pacal Votan, www.13moon.com

8 Housden, Roger, *Sacred Journeys in a Modern World*, Simon and Schuster, 1998

9 Hunbatz Men, *Secrets of Mayan Science and Religion*, Bear and Co., 1990

10 Schele, Linda and David Freidel, *A Forest of Kings: The Untold Story of the Ancient Maya*, William Morrow, New York, 1990

11 Gilbert, Adrian, *The End of Time: The Mayan Prophecies Revisited*, Mainstream, Edinburgh, 2006

12 Calleman, Carl Johan, *The Mayan Calendar and the Transformation of Consciousness*, Bear, Rochester, 2004
13 Jenkins, John Major, *Maya Cosmogenesis 2012*, Bear and Co., Rochester, 1998
14 Birch, Charles, *A Purpose for Everything: Religion in a Postmodern World View*, Twentythird Publications, 1990
15 Capra, Fritjof, *The Tao of Physics*, Flamingo, 1992
16 Benedict, Gerald, *The Mayan Prophecies for 2012*, Watkins, London, 2008
17 Argüelles, José, *Time and the Technosphere*, Bear and Co., 2002
18 Hawking, Stephen, *A Brief History of Time*, Guild, London, 1990
19 Swami Sri Yukteswar, *The Holy Science*, Self-Realisation Fellowship, 2006
20 Pinch, Geraldine, *Egyptian Myth*, Oxford University Press, 2004
21 Assmann, Jan, *The Search for God in Ancient Egypt*, translated by David Lorton, Cornell University, 2001
22 Einstein, Albert, unsourced
23 Benedict, Gerald, *The Mayan Prophecies for 2012*, Watkins, 2008
24 Tedlock, Barbara, *Time and the Highland Maya*, University of New Mexico Press, 1992
25 Schoch, Robert, *Voyages of the Pyramid Builders*, McNally, NY, 2003
26 Coe, Michael D, *Breaking the Maya Code*, Penguin, 1994
27 Fernbank Science Centre, www.fsc.fernbank.edu/

28 Don Isidro, quoted in, Barrios, Carlos, *The Book of Destiny*, HarperOne, New York,2009

29 Leyenaar, Ted, *Ulama: The Perpetuation in Mexico of the Pre-Spanish Ball Game Ullamaliztli*, Leiden, 1978

30 Scarborough, Vernon L and Wilcox, David R (eds), *The Mesoamerican Ballgame*, University of Arizona Press, 1991

31 Schele, Linda and Peter Mathews, *The Code of Kings: The Language of Seven Sacred Maya Temples and Tombs*, Simon and Schuster, NY, 1998

32 Coe, Michael D, *The Maya*, Thames & Hudson, London, 1997

33 Uriarte, Maria Teresa, 'Unity in Duality: The Practice and Symbols of the Mesoamerican Ballgame', in *The Sport of Life and Death: The Mesoamerican Ballgame*, ed. E Michael Whittington, Thames & Hudson, London, 2001

34 Tarnas, Richard, *Cosmos and Psyche, Intimations of a New World View*, Viking Penguin, NY, 2006

35 Martineau, John, *A Little Book of Coincidence in the Solar System*, Wooden, Glastonbury, 2006

36 Bonewitz, Ronald, *Maya Prophecy*, Piatkus, London, 1999

37 Tedlock, Dennis (trans), *Popol Vuh*, Touchstone, NY, 1996

38 Miller, Mary and Karl Taube, *An Illustrated Dictionary of the Gods and Symbols of Ancient Mexico and the Maya*, Thames & Hudson, London, 2003

39 Müller, Max (trans), *The Dhammapada: The Essential Teachings of the Buddha*, Watkins, London, 2006

40 Scaruffi, Piero, *The Nature of Consciousness*, Omniware, 2006

41 James, William, *The Variety of Religious Experience*, Signet, London, 2003

42 Dodd, C H (ed.), *The New English Bible: New Testament*, Oxford and Cambridge University Presses, 1961

43 Christenson, Allen J (trans), *Popol Vuh*, University of Oklahoma Press, 2007

44 Molesky-Poz, Jean, *Contemporary Maya Spirituality: The Ancient Ways are not Lost*, University of Texas Press, 2006

45 Paramahansa Yogananda, *Autobiography of a Yogi*, Rider, London, 1996

46 Council for a Parliament of World Religions, www.cpwr.org

47 The Wisdom Conservancy mission statement, The Wisdom Page www.wisdompage.com/wisdomconservancy.html

48 Otto, Rudolf, *The Idea of the Holy*, translated by John W Harvey, Penguin, 1959

49 Loy, David, *Lack and Transcendence: The Problem of Death and Life in Psychotherapy, Existentialism and Buddhism*, Humanities Press, New Jersey, 1996

50 Kurzweil, Raymond, *The Law of Accelerating Returns*, March 2001, www.kurzweilai.net/

51 Singularity Watch, www.singularitywatch.org

52 Dalai Lama, quoted in *Gentle Bridges: Conversations with the Dalai Lama on the Science of Mind*, Jeremy Hayward and Francisco Varela, Shambhala, 1992

53 Jung, C J, *The Undiscovered Self*, Routledge, London, 1990

54 The Prophets' Conference, www.greatmystery.org/

55 Jowett, Benjamin (trans), *Plato's Dialogues*, 'Timaeus', Bantam, New York, 1986

56 *Space Daily*, 'Chance of a Cometary Impact Re-assessed', 27 Oct 2004 http://www.spacedaily.com/news/asteroid-040.html

57 *Science@NASA*, 'The Sun Does a Flip', 15 Feb 2001 science.nasa.gov/headlines/y2001/ast15feb_1.htm

58 Pinchbeck, Daniel, *2012: The Year of the Mayan Prophecy*, Piatkus, London, 2007

59 Goodall, Dominic, *Hindu Scriptures*, J M Dent, 1996

60 Miller and Taube, *An Illustrated Dictionary of the Gods and Symbols of Ancient Mexico and the Maya*, Thames & Hudson, London, 2003

61 Michaelson, Jay, 'Transformation of Consciousness as Messianic Age: A Nondual, Non-triumphalist View', *Tikkun*, Sept/Oct 2009

62 Scofield, Bruce, 'The Mayan Katun Prophecies', *Alternate Perceptions*, 37, 1996

63 The Wisdom of Kabbalah. www.kabbalah.info

64 Lichtenberg, Georg C, *The Lichtenberg Reader*, 1959 translated and edited by Franz H Mautner and Henry Hatfield, Beacon Press, Boston, 1959

65 Bronowski, J, *Science and Human Values*, New York, Harper Torchbooks, 1956

66 Rogers, Carl, *The Carl Rogers Reader*, ed. Kirshenbaum, Howard, and Henderson, Valerie Land, Constable, London, 1990

67 Bowman, Carol, *Children's Past Lives: How Past Life Memories Affect Your Child*, Bantam, 1997

68 Tucker, Jim, *Life Before Life: A Scientific Investigation of Children's Memories of Previous Lives*, Piatkus, 2009

69 Capra, Fritjof, *The Turning Point: Science, Society, and the Rise of Culture*, Flamingo, 1983

70 Bodhidharma, quoted in *The Wisdom of the Zen Masters*, Timothy Freke, Journey, Hong Kong, 1998

71 Kepler, J, *Epitome of Copernican Astronomy and Harmonies of the World*, Prometheus, 1995